Russian

Rhythms

Learn Through Songs

Vol. 1

lingualism

ISBN: 978-1-962752-12-1

By Artem Orlov and Matthew Aldrich

website: www.lingualism.com

email: contact@lingualism.com

TABLE OF CONTENTS

INTRODUCTION

If you love music and you're learning Russian, this book is for you. With ten original, catchy songs written just for learners, you'll train your ear, boost your vocabulary, and finally start to understand real spoken Russian—while actually enjoying yourself. Whether you're into ballads, pop, rap, or upbeat dance tracks, there's something here for you.

This book is designed for **intermediate learners of Russian (around B1–B2 level)** who want to strengthen their listening skills through engaging, level-appropriate content. Popular Russian music can be a challenge—full of slang, fast speech, and complex grammar that often overwhelms learners. And using commercial songs would have meant dealing with prohibitive, restrictive licensing. So instead, we created something better suited to your needs.

The lyrics were written by Artem Orlov, with the help of AI to explore ideas and phrasing, and the music itself was generated using cutting-edge AI tools. Together, Artem and I (Matthew Aldrich) developed the book's content to guide you through each song, step by step.

The result is a unique listening experience:

- A **range of genres and moods**—from slow ballads to rap, upbeat dance to humorous storytelling.
- A **mix of repeated vocabulary**, to reinforce what you've learned, and **new words** in every track to expand your knowledge.

- A structure that helps you not just "hear" Russian, but actually understand how it works—vocabulary, grammar, and meaning.

We designed this book with **self-learners** in mind. Whether you're learning on your own or supplementing another course, these ten tracks will train your ear, deepen your confidence, and help make Russian feel more natural, musical, and fun.

So grab your headphones, listen often, and enjoy the rhythm of learning!

HOW TO USE THIS BOOK

Each unit of this book is called a **Track**—just like on an album—and takes you through one original song, building your skills step by step. You can go through the tracks in order, as they gradually build listening strategies and reinforce patterns, **or jump around** and start with the songs that interest you most. It's up to you!

Here's how each Track works:

Song Title

A short intro to the title and key concepts in the line—sometimes grammar, sometimes culture, sometimes idioms.

First Listening

You'll listen without reading. Just get a feel for the music and see how much you can catch on your own.

Key Words

We highlight important words and phrases. You'll listen for them, guess meanings, and explore them more deeply—building vocabulary and context awareness.

First Look at the Lyrics

Now it's time to look at the lyrics—and the English translation. Read through the Russian lyrics slowly (with or without the music) and see how much you can figure out from the context. Then, check the English translation to confirm your understanding and fill in any gaps. You might be surprised by how much you've already picked up just by listening! Try to resist the urge to reach for a dictionary—this is a chance to train your intuition and rely on what the song itself gives you.

Breakdown

This is where we go line by line and explain what's happening in the Russian. We break down:

- Grammar points (like verb aspect, cases, and conjugation)
- Vocabulary (including short-form adjectives, reflexive verbs, slang, and more)
- Phrases and structures that might look strange at first—but make sense once explained

Some units include special exercises or quizzes, always with the goal of deepening your understanding and training your ear to listen with more accuracy and confidence.

You'll learn best by listening **more than once**—try shadowing the singer, repeating key lines, and revisiting older tracks as you move forward. The more you listen, the more you'll understand.

Enjoy your journey—and happy listening!

Free Accompanying Audio

Visit www.lingualism.com/audio, **where you can find the free accompanying audio to download or stream.**

TRACK 1

Осталась тень

Song Title

Before listening to the song, let's take a look at the title: **Осталась тень**

- **тень** – This noun means shadow or shade. It is **feminine**, as indicated by the soft sign (**ь**) at the end. Many feminine nouns in Russian end this way.
- **осталась** – This is a **perfective past tense verb**, meaning remained, was left, stayed. It is in the **feminine singular form** because it agrees with the noun **тень**. You may recognize the verb **остаться**, which is a **reflexive verb**.

Word Order in Russian

Unlike English, Russian word order is very flexible. Even though we might expect a sentence like Тень осталась (literally "The shadow has remained"), the words here are reversed. This is a common stylistic choice in Russian, especially in poetry and song lyrics.

Listen for These Lines

When you eventually listen to the song, you'll hear the title **Осталась тень** in the **third line**. Later, in the chorus, you'll hear:

Но лишь тень остаётся у меня.
(But only a shadow remains with me.)

остаётся comes from **оставáться**, the **imperfective** counterpart of **остáться**

The **perfective past tense** suggests something was left behind as a result of a past event.

The **imperfective present tense (остаётся)** describes an ongoing state: the shadow continues to remain.

First Listening

Now, listen to the song. Don't worry if you don't understand everything yet. Instead, focus on recognizing the key lines we looked at above and see how they fit with the melody.

Also, try to catch other basic, familiar words, such as:

твой (your)   **э́то** (this, it)   **нет** (there isn't)

Enjoy the song and see how much you can pick up the first time round!

Key_Words_

Every song has certain words that carry its main emotions and ideas. By focusing on these, you can better understand the song's meaning, even if you don't catch every word. Below are ten important words from Остáлась тень in the exact forms they appear in the lyrics. Many of them appear more than once and help create the song's atmosphere of longing, loss, and memory.

Second Listening

As you listen **for the second time**, don't worry about the meaning. You may already know some of these words, while others may be new to you. In any case, simply **try to catch them as you listen** and check the boxes on the next page:

☐ тепло́   ☐ в пустоте́
☐ в се́рдце   ☐ при́зрак
☐ грусть   ☐ ни судьбу́
☐ дождь   ☐ мечту́
☐ с ве́тром   ☐ откры́та

Even if you don't catch every word right away, just listening for them will help train your ear for Russian. After this step, we'll look at their meanings in more detail!

Understanding the Meanings

Now that you've listened for the words in the song, let's focus on their meanings. Below, you'll see the ten key words in their **base forms** (dictionary form). Next to each word, there's a blank space where you should write the correct English translation.

To help you, a box on the right contains all ten translations, but they are in random order. Match each word with the correct meaning!

Exercise: Write the English translations.

1. тепло́ _____
2. се́рдце _____
3. грусть _____
4. дождь _____
5. ве́тер _____
6. пустота́ _____
7. при́зрак _____
8. судьба́ _____
9. мечта́ _____
10. откры́тый _____

fate
rain
warmth
sadness
heart
emptiness
wind
dream
open
ghost

After you complete the exercise, check your answers below and see how many you got right!

Symbolism in the Song

Now that you know the meanings of the key words, let's go deeper into their symbolism in the song. Below, you'll see the ten words with their English translations. Each word has a deeper meaning in the lyrics, and these explanations are listed in **random order** below and continued on the next page, each labeled with a letter (**A–J**).

Your Task: Match each word to the correct explanation by writing the corresponding letter next to it.

1. **тепло́** – warmth ____
2. **се́рдце** – heart ____
3. **грусть** –sadness ____
4. **дождь** – rain ____
5. **ве́тер** – wind ____
6. **пустота́** –emptiness ____
7. **при́зрак** – ghost ____
8. **судьба́** – fate ____
9. **мечта́** – dream ____
10. **откры́тый** – open ____

Explanation Bank (Random Order)

    A. Captures the emotional core of the lyrics.
    B. Represents the comfort and affection that has now faded into darkness.
    C. Symbolizes fleeting words, memories, and the passage of time.
    D. The final hopeful note, suggesting that despite loss, there is still a chance for return.
    E. Emphasizes the absence and emotional hollowness left behind.
    F. Used in contrast to reality, symbolizing what has been taken away.

G. Tied to the theme of loss and the uncontrollable passage of time.

H. A metaphor for memories that feel real but are no longer tangible.

I. A recurring image linked to loss, longing, and searching.

J. A key symbol of emotion, love, and inner pain.

After completing the exercise, check your answers below and see how well you understood the song's deeper meaning!

Answers: 1. B, 2. J, 3. A, 4. I, 5. C, 6. E, 7. H, 8. G, 9. F, 10. D

Listen Again with Understanding

Now that you've explored the key vocabulary and the deeper meanings behind the lyrics, it's time to listen again, this time with a **new perspective**.

As you listen:

- Pay attention to how these words are used in the song.
- Notice how the emotions and imagery connect to the music.
- Try to hear not just individual words, but the **bigger picture** they create together.

This step will help reinforce your understanding and allow you to experience the song **more fully**.

First Look at the Lyrics

Read Along

Now, let's read the lyrics **while listening to the song**. You're bound to recognize many words that you didn't catch when just listening. That's completely normal! Listening is generally harder than reading in a foreign language, and this step will help reinforce what you've learned.

Refer to the full lyrics at the end of the unit (p. 12) and follow along as you listen again.

Study the Lyrics Without Music

Next, take a moment to read the lyrics **on your own**, without the music. See how much you can understand **without looking at the English translation just yet**.

- Try to recognize words and phrases you've already learned.
- Pay attention to verb forms, noun endings, and word order.
- Don't worry if you don't understand everything yet. This is part of the process!

Study the English Translation

Once you've read through the Russian lyrics, compare them with the **English translation** (on p. 13).

- This will help you understand even more.
- Some words or grammar structures may still be unclear. That's okay!
- You **don't need to match up every word perfectly** at this stage.

Breakdown

In the this section, we'll **analyze the song line by line**. We'll break down:

- **Words and phrases**
- **Grammar points** (gender, cases, verb conjugations, etc.)
- **How the lines fit together in Russian**

This step will **fill in the gaps** and help you **fully grasp** the song's language and meaning!

Verse 1

Я по́мню го́лос твой, как э́хо в пустоте́

- **Я помню** – I remember (1st person singular, present tense)
- **голос твой** – your voice (голос – masculine noun, твой – possessive pronoun for your)
- **как эхо в пустоте** – like an echo in the void
  - **как** – like
  - **пустота** – emptiness or void (feminine noun, used in prepositional case: в пустоте)

Тепло́ твои́х рук раствори́лось в темноте́

- **тепло** – warmth (neuter noun)
- **твоих рук** – your hands (рука – hand is feminine; here in genitive plural: of your hands)
- **растворилось** – dissolved (past tense, neuter singular, referring to тепло)
- **в темноте** – in the darkness (темнота – darkness, in prepositional case)

Оста́лась тень от на́ших дней

- **Осталась** – remained (past tense, feminine, agreeing with тень)
- **тень** – shadow (feminine noun)
- **от наших дней** – from our days (дней is genitive plural of день, day)

А в се́рдце то́лько дождь и грусть тепе́рь

- **в сердце** – in (my) heart (сердце is neuter, prepositional case)
- **только дождь и грусть теперь** – only rain and sadness now
  - **дождь** – rain (masculine noun)
  - **грусть** – sadness (feminine noun)
  - **теперь** – now (contrasts past happiness with current sorrow)

Chorus

Ты ушла́, и мне не верну́ть

- **Ты ушла** – You left (past tense, ушла is feminine form of уйти)
- **и мне не вернуть** – and I can't bring (it) back
  - **вернуть** – to return, bring back (infinitive)
  - **мне не вернуть** – impersonal structure meaning I cannot return (it) (literally "to me, it is not returnable")

Все слова́, что с ве́тром улете́ли в ночь

- **все слова** – all the words (слова – plural form of слово, word)

- **что с ветром улетели в ночь** – that flew away with the wind into the night
  - **с ветром** – with the wind (instrumental case)
  - **улетели** – flew away (past tense, plural, agreeing with слова)
  - **в ночь** – into the night (accusative case)

Я ищу́ тебя́ в ка́плях дождя́

- **Я ищу** – I search for (1st person singular, present tense)
- **тебя** – you (accusative case)
- **в каплях дождя** – in the drops of rain
  - **каплях** – drops (prepositional plural of капля)
  - **дождя** – of rain (genitive singular of дождь)

Но лишь тень остаётся у меня́

- **но лишь тень** – but only a shadow
- **остаётся у меня** – remains with me
  - **остаётся** – remains, stays (present tense, 3rd person singular)
  - **у меня** – with me (possessive structure using y + genitive)

Verse 2

Когда́-то мир был по́лон све́та и огня́

- **Когда-то** – Once (in the past)
- **мир был полон света и огня** – the world was full of light and fire
  - **полон** – full of (short-form adjective, agreeing with мир)
  - **света и огня** – of light and fire (both in genitive case)

Но без тебя́ здесь нет ни со́лнца, ни дня

- **Но без тебя** – But without you
- **здесь нет ни солнца, ни дня** – there is neither sun nor day here
    - **ни... ни...** – neither... nor...
    - **нет** – there is no (requires genitive case: солнца, дня)

Я закрыва́ю глаза́, ви́жу твой силуэ́т

- **Я закрываю глаза** – I close my eyes
- **вижу твой силуэт** – I see your silhouette
    - **вижу** – I see (1st person singular)
    - **силуэт** – silhouette (masculine noun)

Но э́то при́зрак, э́то не ты... бо́льше нет

- **Но это призрак** – But it's a ghost
- **это не ты... больше нет** – It's not you... (you're) no longer here

Bridge

Зна́ешь, я не виню́ ни тебя́, ни судьбу́

- **Знаешь** – You know (2nd person singular, present tense)
- **я не виню ни тебя, ни судьбу** – I don't blame either you or fate
    - **виню** – I blame (1st person singular, present)
    - **судьбу** – fate (accusative case of судьба)

Про́сто вре́мя течёт, забира́я мечту́

- **Просто время течёт** – Time just flows
- **забирая мечту** – taking the dream away
- **забирая** – taking away (present participle, active)

- **мечту** – dream (accusative case of **мечта**)

Но е́сли вдруг ты вспо́мнишь меня́

- **Но если вдруг** – But if suddenly
- **ты вспомнишь меня** – you remember me (**вспомнишь** –
  2nd person singular, future/present)

Моя́ дверь для тебя́ откры́та всегда́...

- **Моя дверь** – My door
- **для тебя открыта всегда** – is always open for you
  - **открыта** – open (short-form adjective, feminine)

Lyrics

Куплет 1

Я по́мню го́лос твой, как э́хо в пустоте́,

Тепло́ твои́х рук раствори́лось в темноте́.

Оста́лась тень от на́ших дней,

А в се́рдце то́лько дождь и грусть тепе́рь.

Припе́в

Ты ушла́, и мне не верну́ть

Все слова́, что с ве́тром улете́ли в ночь.

Я ищу́ тебя́ в ка́плях дождя́,

Но лишь тень остаётся у меня́.

Куплет 2

Когда́-то мир был по́лон све́та и огня́,

Но без тебя́ здесь нет ни со́лнца, ни дня.

Я закрыва́ю глаза́, ви́жу твой силуэ́т,

Но э́то при́зрак, э́то не ты... бо́льше нет.

(Припе́в)

Зна́ешь, я не виню́ ни тебя́, ни судьбу́,

Про́сто вре́мя течёт, забира́я мечту́.

Но е́сли вдруг ты вспо́мнишь меня́,

Моя́ дверь для тебя́ откры́та всегда́...

(Припе́в)

Translation

Verse 1

I remember your voice, like an echo in the void,

The warmth of your hands dissolved into the dark.

Only a shadow remains from our days,

And in my heart, only rain and sorrow now.

Chorus

You left, and I can't bring back

All the words that flew away with the wind into the night.

I search for you in the drops of rain,

But only a shadow remains with me.

Verse 2

Once the world was full of light and fire,

But without you, there is no sun, no day.

I close my eyes, I see your silhouette,

But it's just a ghost, it's not you... not anymore.

(Chorus)

Bridge

You know, I don't blame you or fate,

Time just flows, taking dreams away.

But if one day you remember me,

My door will always be open for you...

(Chorus)

TRACK 2

Ну и ладно!

Song Title_

This song is playful, upbeat, and full of everyday frustrations turned into reasons to shrug and smile. The title **Ну и ла́дно!** can be translated in lots of ways: Oh well!, Whatever!, Let it go!, or No big deal! It's the kind of thing you say when you decide not to stress over the little things.

Not Just Words. It's an Idiom!

At first glance, **"Ну и ла́дно!"** might seem like just a string of basic words, but together, they form a **common idiom** that doesn't quite translate literally. Let's break it down **word by word** first, then look at the epression as a whole.

- **Ну** – A filler word, similar to well or so in English.
  Eample: Ну, пойдём! – "Well, let's go!"
- **и** – This is the basic conjunction and that you probably already know.
  Eample: Мама и папа – "Mom and Dad"
- **ла́дно** – A fleible word that can mean okay, fine, alright, depending on the contet.
  Eample: Ла́дно, я согласен – "Alright, I agree."

When learning a language, it's important to remember that idioms can't be understood by translating each word individually. Even if you know all the words in a phrase, the meaning as a whole may be completely different.

"Ну и ла́дно!" is one of those phrases. Word for word, it looks simple: "well and okay." But together, it forms an idiomatic epression.

It carries the tone of brushing something off or deciding not to stress about it. Like many idioms, it needs to be learned and remembered as a set phrase, not pieced together word by word.

Other Similar Phrases in the Song

The song features several other phrases with a similar "whatever, it's fine" attitude. These are all idiomatic epressions, so their **real meaning is different from the literal translation**. Pay attention to how they're used in contet:

- **Ну и пусть!** – So what! / Let it be!
  (literally "Well and let [it]")
- **Эх, что поде́лать!** – Eh, what can you do!
  (literally "Eh, what to do")
- **Ай, да ла́дно!** – Ah, whatever!
  (literally "Λh, yes okay")
- **Ну и что?** – So what?
  (literally "Well and what?")
- **Ничего́ стра́шного!** – No big deal!
  (literally "Nothing scary")
- **Фиг с ним!** – Screw it! (colloquial)
  (literally "A fig with him") – a very informal way of saying "Forget it" or "Whatever!"

As you listen to the song for the **first time**, your goal isn't to understand every word; it's to start recognizing the **tone and key phrases**. This song is packed with **idiomatic epressions** that don't translate literally, so your task is to **spot the difference** between what the words literally say and what they actually mean.

Listen for the phrases below. They may sound familiar now that you've read about them, but hearing them in real-time can still be tricky. That's part of the challenge!

As you listen, **check the bo** when you hear each one:

☐ **Ну и ла́дно!** (Well and okay → Oh well!)

☐ **Ну и пусть!** (Well and let [it] → So what!)

☐ **Эх, что поде́лать!** (Eh, what to do → What can you do!)

☐ **Ай, да ла́дно!** (Ah, yes okay → Whatever!)

☐ **Ну и что?** (Well and what? → So what?)

☐ **Ничего́ стра́шного!** (Nothing scary → No big deal!)

☐ **Фиг с ним!** (A fig with him → Screw it!)

Focus on their **sound**, **rhythm**, and **emotion**. That's often the first step in truly understanding idiomatic language.

Key Words

Some words in this song may be new to you, while others you might recognize but not have caught by ear before. These words appear in meaningful or repeated parts of the lyrics and help capture the overall mood: light, humorous, and a little chaotic.

As you listen **for the second time**, don't worry about understanding everything. Just try to **catch these words or phrases as they appear** and **check them off** when you hear them.

- ☐ **опозда́ла** (was late)
- ☐ **зонт** (umbrella)
- ☐ **под дождём** (in the rain)
- ☐ **стресс** (stress)
- ☐ **ко́фе** (coffee)
- ☐ **сюрпри́з** (surprise)
- ☐ **сда́чи** (change – money)
- ☐ **разряди́лся** (died / lost charge)
- ☐ **улыбни́сь** (smile!)
- ☐ **жизнь** (life)

You'll probably hear some of these more than once. See how many you can catch without looking at the lyrics!

First Look at the Lyrics

Gap Fill

In this activity, you'll get your first look at the song's lyrics. Some words have been removed. Your task is to **listen and try to fill in the missing words** as you hear them in the song.

Each blank is numbered to help you check your answers later.
Don't look at the word bank yet. (It's at the bottom of the page.)
Just focus on what you hear.

After your first attempt, go to the net page, check the word bank,
and **listen again** to fill in any blanks you may have missed.

Куплéт 1

Опоздáла на ___(1) – ну и пусть!

Зонт забы́ла под дождём – эх, что подéлать!

На ___(2) снóва стресс – ну и лáдно, ну и лáдно!

Кóфе пролилá ___(3) – ай, да лáдно!

Припéв

Бывáет, ну и что?

Ничегó стрáшного!

Жизнь – игрá, а я в ___(4) королéва, ха-ха-ха!

Фиг с ним, ну и пусть,

___(5) не мóжет быть ___(6) в скáзке, ну и пусть!

Куплéт 2

Сосéд ___(7) шуми́т – ну и лáдно!

Кот надéлал мне сюрпри́з – эх, что подéлать!

В ___(8) нéту сдáчи – ну и пусть, ну и пусть!

Телефóн разряди́лся – ай, да лáдно!

Бридж

Éсли ___(9) не везёт, прóсто улыбни́сь,

Мир большóй, но ___(10) у меня́ есть жизнь!

Word Bank

автóбус • вдруг • всё • затó • как • магази́не •
ней • опя́ть • рабóте • снóва

You can check your answers on page 22.

Breakdown

Now let's look closely at how the Russian works, one line at a time.

Опозда́ла на авто́бус – ну и пусть!

- **опоздала** – was late (past tense, feminine, from опоздать)
- **на автобус** – for the bus (на + accusative)
- **ну и пусть** – so what / let it be (idiomatic)

Зонт забы́ла под дождём – эх, что поде́лать!

- **зонт** – umbrella (masculine noun)
- **забыла** – forgot (past tense, feminine)
- **под дождём** – in the rain (дождь in instrumental case)
- **эх, что поделать** – eh, what can you do! (idiomatic expression of resignation)

На рабо́те сно́ва стресс – ну и ла́дно, ну и ла́дно!

- **на работе** – at work (prepositional case)
- **снова** – again
- **стресс** – stress (borrowed word, masculine)
- **ну и ладно** – oh well! (repeated for emphasis)

Ко́фе пролила́ опя́ть – ай, да ла́дно!

- **кофе** – coffee (indeclinable noun, usually masculine)
- **пролила** – spilled (past tense, feminine)
- **опять** – again
- **ай, да ладно** – ah, whatever!

Быва́ет, ну и что?

- **быва́ет** – it happens (3rd person singular, present tense)
- **ну и что?** – so what? (idiomatic)
- **Ничего́ стра́шного!**
- **ничего страшного** – no big deal! (literally "nothing scary")

Жизнь – игра́, а я в ней короле́ва, ха-ха-ха!

- **жизнь** – life (feminine noun)
- **игра** – game (feminine noun)
- **в ней** – in it (prepositional case, feminine)
- **королева** – queen (feminine noun)

Фиг с ним, ну и пусть!

- **фиг с ним** – screw it / whatever! (very colloquial)
- **ну и пусть** – let it be (same idiom as earlier)

Всё не мо́жет быть как в ска́зке, ну и пусть!

- **всё не может быть** – not everything can be
- **как в сказке** – like in a fairy tale (prepositional case)
- **ну и пусть** – let it be

Verse 2

Сосе́д сно́ва шуми́т – ну и ла́дно!

- **сосед** – neighbor (masculine noun)
- **снова** – again
- **шумит** – is being noisy / makes noise (3rd person singular, present)
- **ну и ладно** – oh well!

Кот наде́лал мне сюрпри́з – эх, что поде́лать!

- **кот** – cat (masculine noun)
- **наделал** – (he) made (in this context, slang for pooped/messed)
- **мне сюрприз** – a surprise for me
- **эх, что поделать!** – eh, what can you do!

В магази́не не́ту сда́чи – ну и пусть, ну и пусть!

- **в магазине** – in the store (prepositional case)
- **нету сдачи** – there is no change (сдача – change, genitive)
- **ну и пусть** – so what!

Телефо́н разряди́лся – ай, да ла́дно!

- **телефон** – phone (masculine noun)
- **разрядился** – ran out of battery (past tense, masculine)
- **ай, да ладно!** – ah, whatever!

Bridge

Éсли вдруг не везёт, про́сто улыбни́сь

- **если вдруг** – if suddenly / if by chance
- **не везёт** – (I/you) have bad luck / things aren't going well
- **просто улыбнись** – just smile (улыбнись – imperative, 2nd person singular)

Мир большо́й, но зато́ у меня́ есть жизнь!

- **мир большой** – the world is big
- **но зато** – but at least / but still
- **у меня есть жизнь** – I have life (literally "life exists with me")

Lyrics

Ну и ладно!

Куплéт 1

Опоздáла на автóбус – ну и пусть!

Зонт забы́ла под дождём – эх, что подéлать!

На рабóте снóва стресс – ну и лáдно, ну и лáдно!

Кóфе пролилá опя́ть – ай, да лáдно!

припéв

Бывáет, ну и что?

Ничегó стрáшного!

Жизнь – игрá, а я в ней королéва, ха-ха-ха!

Фиг с ним, ну и пусть,

Всё не мóжет быть как в скáзке, ну и пусть!

Куплéт 2

Сосéд снóва шуми́т – ну и лáдно!

Кот надéлал мне сюрпри́з – эх, что подéлать!

В магази́не нéту сдáчи – ну и пусть, ну и пусть!

Телефóн разряди́лся – ай, да лáдно!

(Припéв)

Бридж

Éсли вдруг не везёт, прóсто улыбни́сь,

Мир большóй, но затó у меня́ есть жизнь!

(Припéв)

Translation

Verse 1

Missed the bus – so what?

Forgot my umbrella in the rain – eh, what can you do!

Stressed at work again – oh well, oh well!

Spilled my coffee again – ah, whatever!

Chorus

It happens, so what?

No big deal!

Life's a game, and I'm the queen, ha-ha-ha!

Screw it, let it be,

Not everything can be a fairytale, so let it be!

Verse 2

Neighbor's loud again – oh well!

My cat left me a surprise – eh, what can you do!

No change at the store – so what, so what!

My phone just died – ah, whatever!

(Chorus)

Bridge

If luck runs out, just smile,

The world is big, but at least I'm alive!

(Chorus)

TRACK 3

Танцуй, как хочешь!

Song Title

The title **Танцуй, как хóчешь!** literally means:

- **Танцуй** – Dance! (imperative of танцевать)
- **как хочешь** – how you want (literally "as you want"; хочешь is the 2nd person singular present of хотеть – to want)

Put together, the phrase means: **"Dance how you want!"**
It's a clear command, but also an expression of **freedom, individuality, and confidence.** The title sets the tone for the entire song: be yourself, move your way, ignore the rules.

First Listening

This song is packed with **imperative verbs** (commands) that encourage action, movement, and self-expression. As you listen for the **first time**, focus on **hearing the commands** and **check them off** when you hear them:

- ☐ **Идú** – Go / walk!
- ☐ **Слýшай** – Listen!
- ☐ **Забýдь** – Forget!
- ☐ **Ловú** – Catch!
- ☐ **Танцýй** – Dance!
- ☐ **Двúгай** – Move!
- ☐ **Не прячь** – Don't hide!
- ☐ **Не смотрú** – Don't look!

Try to notice how these verbs **sound**, their **intonation**, **stress**, and the way they drive the rhythm of the song. They aren't just grammar; they carry emotion.

Key Words

Every song has words that carry its **main message and energy**. In Танцуй, как хо́чешь!, those words are all about **movement, confidence, and self-expression**. By focusing on them, you'll begin to feel the pulse of the song, even if you don't understand every word yet.

Second Listening

As you listen **for the second time**, try to catch the following phrases and words **in the exact forms they appear in the lyrics**. Some may be familiar, some brand new, and that's okay! Just **listen and check the box** when you hear each one:

☐ жми на старт
☐ не жди назад
☐ сделай шаг
☐ лета́ть
☐ мне всё равно́

☐ не прячь ого́нь
☐ ты я́ркий
☐ забу́дь запре́ты
☐ сильне́й шаги́
☐ лови́ свобо́ду

Even if you don't catch all of them, this exercise helps train your ear to hear how Russian sounds in real time.

Now let's look at the same ten words and phrases in their **base (dictionary) forms**. Write the English translation for each. Use the word bank to the right (translations are listed in random order).

Exercise: Write the English Translations

1. жать _____
2. ждать _____
3. шаг _____
4. летáть _____
5. всё равнó _____
6. прятáть _____
7. я́ркий _____
8. запрéт _____
9. си́льный _____
10. лови́ть _____

ban / restriction
bright
it doesn't matter
step
strong
to catch
to fly
to hide
to press
to wait

First Look at the Lyrics

Let's take your first pass through the song's lyrics, step by step. Don't worry about grammar or full comprehension yet. This is about getting familiar with the sound and flow of the language.

Step 1: Listen and Read Along

Turn to the lyrics on page 33. Listen to the song while reading the Russian lyrics.
Just follow along. Don't try to translate or pause. Let the words flow with the music.

Step 2: Read Without Music

Now read through the lyrics **slowly and carefully** on your own, without the audio.

- Underline or circle words you recognize.
- Try to get a sense of the meaning, even if it's just a few lines or phrases.
- Don't look at the English yet.

Step 3: Compare with the English Translation

Now check the English translation (page 34) and see how much you understood.

You might not match up every word. That's completely normal.

Focus on:

- Which parts you got right
- Any new phrases or expressions you find interesting
- How the Russian wording compares to the English meaning

This process helps build your confidence and prepares you for a deeper breakdown in the next section.

Breakdown

Now let's look closely at how the Russian works, one line at a time.

In this section, we'll look at:

- Key vocabulary and phrases
- Grammar points (verb tense, noun cases, etc.)

- How the lines are structured and why they work in Russian

Verse 1

Жми на старт, не жди наза́д

- **жми** – press! (imperative of жать)
- **на старт** – the start ("на" + accusative)
- **не жди** – don't wait (imperative of ждать)
- **назад** – back, backwards

Мир большо́й – твой звездопа́д!

- **мир** – world (masculine noun)
- **большой** – big (adjective, masculine)
- **твой** – your (possessive pronoun)
- **звездопад** – meteor shower (literally "a fall of stars")

Не бо́йся, сде́лай шаг

- **не бойся** – don't be afraid (imperative, reflexive verb from бояться)
- **сделай** – make, do (imperative of сделать)
- **шаг** – a step (masculine noun)

Кто сказа́л, что не мо́жешь лета́ть?

- **кто сказал** – who said
- **что не можешь** – that you can't (можешь – 2nd person singular of мочь)
- **летать** – to fly (imperfective infinitive)

Пусть смею́тся – мне всё равно́

- **пусть смеются** – let them laugh (пусть + 3rd person plural)
- **мне всё равно** – I don't care (literally "it's all the same to me")

Я живу́, как в кино́

- **я живу** – I live (1st person singular, present)
- **как в кино** – like in a movie ("в кино" = in the movies)

Пусть говоря́т: «Ты не тако́й!»

- **пусть говорят** – let them say
- **ты не такой** – you're not like them (такой – such / like that)

Но мой сти́ль – мой поко́й!

- **мой стиль** – my style
- **мой покой** – my peace / calm

Chorus

Танцу́й, как хо́чешь! Дви́гай, как мо́жешь!

- **танцуй** – dance! (imperative of танцевать)
- **как хочешь** – how you want (2nd person singular of хотеть)
- **двигай** – move! (imperative of двигать)
- **как можешь** – how you can (2nd person singular of мочь)

Не прячь ого́нь, ты я́ркий, ты мо́жешь!

- **не прячь** – don't hide! (imperative of прятать)
- **огонь** – fire (masculine noun)

- **ты яркий** – you are bright (adjective)
- **ты можешь** – you can (2nd person singular of мочь)

Не смотри́ вниз, сме́ло иди́

- **не смотри** – don't look (imperative of смотреть)
- **вниз** – down
- **смело** – boldly (adverb)
- **иди** – go / walk (imperative of идти)

Мир за тобо́й – про́сто гори́!

- **мир за тобой** – the world is behind you
- **просто гори** – just burn! (гори – imperative of гореть; metaphorically: shine, blaze)

Verse 2

Слу́шай бит, забу́дь запре́ты

- **слушай** – listen! (imperative of слушать)
- **бит** – beat (borrowed word)
- **забудь** – forget! (imperative of забыть)
- **запреты** – restrictions / bans (plural of запрет)

Знай, твои́ ри́тмы – э́то отве́ты!

- **знай** – know! (imperative of знать)
- **твои ритмы** – your rhythms
- **это ответы** – these are the answers

Вы́ше звук, сильне́й шаги́

- **выше** – higher (comparative of высокий)
- **звук** – sound
- **сильней** – stronger (comparative of сильный)
- **шаги** – steps (plural of шаг)

Ты живёшь – и э́то моти́в!

- **ты живёшь** – you are alive / you live
- **это мотив** – this is the motive / reason

Bridge

Лови́ свобо́ду – раз, два, три!

- **лови** – catch! (imperative of ловить)
- **свободу** – freedom (accusative of свобода)
- **раз, два, три** – one, two, three (count-in for rhythm)

Звук гро́мче, смеле́е внутри́!

- **звук громче** – sound louder (comparative)
- **смелее** – bolder (comparative of смелый)
- **внутри** – inside

Нет грани́ц, нет пра́вил тут

- **нет границ** – there are no boundaries (границы – genitive plural)
- **нет правил** – there are no rules (правила – genitive plural)
- **тут** – here

Ты – ого́нь, пусть все пойму́т!

- **ты – огонь** – you are fire
- **пусть все поймут** – let everyone understand! (пусть + 3rd person plural of понять)

Lyrics

Куплéт 1

Жми на старт, не жди назáд,

Мир большóй – твой звездопáд!

Не бóйся, сдéлай шáг,

Кто сказáл, что не мóжешь летáть?

Предприпéв

Пусть смею́тся – мне всё равнó,

Я живý, как в кинó!

Пусть говоря́т: «Ты не такóй!»

Но мой стиль – мой покóй!

Припéв

Танцýй, как хóчешь! Двúгай, как мóжешь!

Не прячь огóнь, ты я́ркий, ты мóжешь!

Не смотрú вниз, смéло идú,

Мир за тобóй – прóсто горú!

Куплéт 2

Слýшай бит, забýдь запрéты,

Знай, твой рúтмы – э́то отвéты!

Вы́ше звук, сильнéй шагú,

Ты живёшь – и э́то мотúв!

(Предприпéв + Припéв)

Бридж

Ловú свобóду – раз, два, три!

Звук грóмче, смелéе внутрú!

Нет гранúц, нет прáвил тут,

Ты – огóнь, пусть все поймýт!   (Припéв) (х2)

Translation

Verse 1

Press start, don't look back,

The world is big – your starry fall!

Don't be afraid, just take a step,

Who said that you can't fly?

Pre-Chorus

Let them laugh – I don't care,

I live like in a movie!

Let them say, "You're not like them,"

But my style is my peace!

Chorus

Dance how you want! Move how you can!

Don't hide your fire, you're bright, you can!

Don't look down, walk boldly ahead,

The world is behind you – just burn!

Verse 2

Listen to the beat, forget the bans,

Know that your rhythms are the answers!

Turn up the sound, step stronger,

You are alive – and that's the motive!

(Pre-Chorus + Chorus)

Bridge

Catch your freedom – one, two, three!

The sound is louder, be bolder inside!

No limits, no rules here,

You're the fire – let them see! (Chorus) (x2)

TRACK 4

Вместе навсегда

Song_Title_

The title **Вместе навсегда** means **"Together Forever."** It's made up of two key adverbs:

- **вместе** – together
  - This adverb describes doing something **with someone**, in the same place or as a unit.
  - Example: Мы вместе гуляем. – We are walking together.
- **навсегда** – forever
  - This adverb expresses **permanence**, something that will last for all time.
  - It's made up of на (for) + всегда (always).

Together, they carry a deep emotional meaning: a promise of lasting connection, no matter what.

Other Useful Adverbs in the Song

This song is full of **adverbs of time, place, and degree**, the kinds of words that give **emotion, rhythm, and nuance** to how we describe actions.

Here are a few you'll hear:

- **рядом** – nearby, close by
  Она всегда рядом со мной. – She's always close by.
- **вместе** – together
  Мы работаем вместе. – We work together.

- **навсегда́** – forever

  Они остану́тся вме́сте навсегда́. – They will stay together forever.

- **за́втра** – tomorrow

  Я уви́жусь с ней за́втра. – I'll see her tomorrow.

- **вновь** – again

  Мы встре́тились вновь. – We met again.

- **вдали́** – in the distance

  Мы ви́дели го́ры вдали́. – We saw mountains in the distance.

- **день за днём** – day by day

  Мы стро́им э́то день за днём. – We're building it day by day.

- **ве́чно** – eternally, always

  Я бу́ду тебя́ ве́чно люби́ть. – I will love you forever.

You don't need to memorize them all now; just be aware of them as you listen. These words help build the **poetic, emotional feel** of the song.

First Listening

Now listen to the song **for the first time**, and answer these **True or False** questions based on what you hear. Don't worry about catching every word. Just try to get the **main ideas and images**.

Check True (✔) or False (✖):

1. ____ The singer says her voice brings peace to her partner.
2. ____ She describes seeing their home filled with joy.
3. ____ She says they'll be together forever, even through storms.
4. ____ She talks about holding hands while walking through a forest.

5. ___ She says they'll meet again, no matter where they are.

6. ___ She compares their love to something eternal.

7. ___ She says they've already built a home together.

8. ___ She describes stars shining for them in the distance.

Answer Key: 1. False — The singer does not mention her own voice; she describes his voice as music in her heart. 2. True — She sees their home and the two of them full of joy. 3. True — She says they'll be together "tomorrow and always" and mentions rain and wind, saying nothing can stop them. 4. False — There is no mention of holding hands or walking through a forest. 5. True — She says they'll meet again wherever they are. 6. True — She calls their love eternal ("вечная любовь"). 7. False — She sings that they will build a home together, but they haven't yet. 8. True — She describes the stars shining for them in the distance.

Key Words

In this song, many of the important words are described with strong emotional or poetic language, like "eternal love" or "music in my heart." The exercise on the following page helps you notice **how these words are used in context** and what they're paired with.

Match each **key noun** from the song with the **phrase or adjective** that goes with it. All of these combinations are taken directly from the lyrics.

You may write the letter of the match next to each noun.

Exercise: Match the Word to Its Description or Partner (in the forms used in the lyrics)

1. любо́вь (love) → _____
2. жизнь (life) → _____
3. се́рдце (heart) → _____
4. го́лос (voice) → _____
5. дом (home) → _____
6. нас (us) → _____
7. дождь и ве́тер (rain and wind) → _____
8. звёзды (stars) → _____
9. ты (you) → _____
10. доро́ги (roads) → _____

Phrase/Description Bank (Random Order)

A. му́зыка в моём се́рце
B. тепло́ сия́ет
C. бесконе́чно
D. све́тят нам вдали́
E. не́жная, ве́чная
F. нам всё нипочём
G. нас, по́лных ра́дости
H. моя́ си́ла, наде́жда, жела́ние
I. в се́рдце моём
J. мо́гут нас пу́тать

Answer Key: 1. E, 2. C, 3. I, 4. A, 5. B, 6. G, 7. F, 8. D, 9. H, 10. J

—

First Look at the Lyrics

Before we analyze the song in detail, take a moment to get familiar with the lyrics. Don't worry about understanding everything right away. This is about getting a feel for the sound, flow, and mood of the song.

Step 1: Listen and Read Along

Turn to the Russian lyrics on page 43.

- Play the song and follow along with the words.
- Just listen and read, no need to pause or translate.

Step 2: Read Without Music

Now read the lyrics again, this time without the music.

- Go slowly and try to spot words or phrases you recognize.
- Underline anything that stands out or repeats.
- Don't look at the English translation yet.

Step 3: Compare with the English Translation

Turn to the English translation (page 44) and compare it line by line with the Russian.

- See how much you understood.
- Look for any new words or expressions you want to remember.
- Notice how meaning is expressed differently in Russian and English.

You're now ready to go deeper into the lyrics in the Breakdown section.

Breakdown

Now let's look closely at how the Russian works, one line at a time.

In this section, we'll look at:

- Key vocabulary and phrases
- Grammar points (verb tense, noun cases, etc.)
- How the lines are structured and why they work in Russian

Verse 1

Когда́ ты ря́дом – мир я́рче, чем со́лнце

- **когда** – when (used to indicate time)
- **ты рядом** – you are near; рядом = near, nearby (adverb)
- **мир** – world (masculine noun)
- **ярче** – brighter (comparative form of яркий – bright)
- **чем** – than (used for comparisons)
- **солнце** – sun (neuter noun)

Твой го́лос — му́зыка в моём се́рце

- **твой** – your (masculine, agrees with **голос**)
- **голос** – voice (masculine noun)
- **музыка** – music (feminine noun)
- **в моём сердце** – in my heart (prepositional case)
    - **моём** – my (prepositional masculine/neuter form, agrees with сердце)
    - **сердце** – heart (neuter noun)

Я закрыва́ю глаза́ и начина́ю смея́ться

- **я закрываю** – I close (1st person singular, present tense of **закрывать**)

- **глаза** – eyes (plural, accusative case)
- **и** – and
- **начинаю** – I begin (1st person singular, present tense of **начинать**)
- **смеяться** – to laugh (reflexive verb, infinitive)

Вижу наш дом, нас, полных радости

- **вижу** – I see (1st person singular, present tense of видеть)
- **наш дом** – our home (accusative case)
- **нас** – us (accusative case)
- **полных радости** – full of joy
  - **полных** – full of (plural genitive adjective agreeing with нас)
  - **радости** – of joy (genitive singular of радость)

Chorus

Мы будем вместе — завтра и вечно

- **мы будем** – we will be (future tense of быть)
- **вместе** – together (adverb)
- **завтра и вечно** – tomorrow and forever (adverbs of time)

Пусть дождь и ветер, нам всё нипочём!

- **пусть** – let (used to express encouragement or concession)
- **дождь и ветер** – rain and wind (both masculine nouns)
- **нам** – to us (dative case of мы)
- **всё нипочём** – nothing bothers us (idiomatic expression; literally "everything is of no consequence")

Рядом с тобой — жизнь бесконечно

- **рядом с тобой** – next to you / with you (instrumental case)

- **жизнь** – life (feminine noun)
- **бесконечно** – endlessly / without end (adverb)

Тепло́ сия́ет в се́рдце моём

- **тепло** – warmth (neuter noun)
- **сияет** – shines (3rd person singular, present tense of **сиять**)
- **в сердце моём** – in my heart (prepositional case; poetic word order)

Verse 2

Доро́ги мо́гут нас пу́тать, но зна́ем

- **дороги** – roads (plural of дорога, feminine)
- **могут** – can (3rd person plural of мочь)
- **нас** – us (accusative case)
- **путать** – to confuse (infinitive)
- **но знаем** – but we know (1st person plural, present tense of **знать**)

Где бы мы ни бы́ли — встре́тимся вновь

- **где бы мы ни были** – wherever we may be (subjunctive construction)
  - **были** – were (past tense, plural)
- **встретимся** – we will meet (future tense, reflexive verb **встретиться**)
- **вновь** – again (synonym for снова)

Ты — моя́ си́ла, наде́жда, жела́ние

- **ты** – you
- **моя сила** – my strength (feminine noun)
- **надежда** – hope (feminine noun)

- **желание** – desire (neuter noun)

Ты — моя́ ве́чная, не́жная любо́вь

- **моя** – my (feminine form, agrees with любовь)
- **вечная, нежная** – eternal, gentle (feminine adjectives)
- **любовь** – love (feminine noun)

Bridge

Смотри́, как звёзды нам све́тят вдали́

- **смотри** – look (imperative, 2nd person singular)
- **звёзды** – stars (plural of звезда, feminine)
- **светят** – shine (3rd person plural of светить)
- **нам** – to us (dative)
- **вдали** – in the distance (adverb)

Бу́ду с тобо́й — навсегда́, как мечта́ли

- **буду** – I will be (future tense of быть)
- **с тобой** – with you (instrumental case)
- **навсегда** – forever
- **как мечтали** – as we dreamed (past tense, plural of мечтать)

Ночь и рассве́т, день за днём

- **ночь и рассвет** – night and dawn (feminine and masculine nouns)
- **день за днём** – day after day (idiomatic phrase)

Мы наш дом постро́им вдвоём

- **мы построим** – we will build (future tense of построить)
- **наш дом** – our home (accusative case)
- **вдвоём** – the two of us together (adverbial expression from два, meaning "just the two")

Lyrics

Куплет 1

Когда́ ты ря́дом — мир я́рче, чем со́лнце,

Твой го́лос — му́зыка в моём се́рце.

Я закрыва́ю глаза́ и начина́ю смея́ться,

Ви́жу наш дом, нас, по́лных ра́дости.

припе́в

Мы бу́дем вме́сте — за́втра и ве́чно,

Пусть дождь и ве́тер, нам всё нипочём!

Ря́дом с тобо́й — жизнь бесконе́чно

Тепло́ сия́ет в се́рдце моём.

Куплет 2

Доро́ги мо́гут нас пу́тать, но зна́ем,

Где бы мы ни бы́ли — встре́тимся вновь.

Ты — моя́ си́ла, наде́жда, жела́ние,

Ты — моя́ ве́чная, не́жная любо́вь.

(Припе́в)

Бридж

Смотри́, как звёзды нам све́тят вдали́,

Бу́ду с тобо́й — навсегда́, как мечта́ли.

Ночь и рассве́т, день за днём,

Мы наш дом постро́им вдвоём.

(Припе́в)

Translation

Verse 1

When you're near, the world shines brighter than the sun,

Your voice is music in my heart.

I close my eyes and laugh,

I see our home and us full of joy.

Chorus

We'll be together, tomorrow and always,

Through rain and wind, nothing can stop us!

With you beside me, life is forever

Warmth shines in my heart.

Verse 2

The roads may try to confuse us, but we know,

Wherever we are, we'll meet again.

You are my strength, my hope, my desire,

You are my eternal, gentle love.

(Chorus)

Bridge

Look how the stars are shining for us,

I'll be with you, forever, just as we dreamed.

Night and dawn, day by day,

We'll build our home, just us two.

(Chorus)

TRACK 5

Жизнь на районе

Song Title

The title of this song, **Жизнь на райóне**, literally means **"Life in the Hood."** But to fully understand its meaning (and its tone), we need to look more closely at the grammar and slang behind the phrase.

На районе vs. В районе

In standard Russian, the phrase would usually be:

в районе – in the district / neighborhood

But here, the song uses **на районе**—a **nonstandard, slangy version**.

Why is this important? Because **switching the preposition from "в" (in) to "на" (on)** changes more than just the grammar. It changes the **feel** of the word **район**.

- **в районе** is neutral and formal, how you'd describe a neighborhood on a map or in a real estate ad.
- **на районе** is informal and rooted in **urban slang**. It's how people from the streets talk about their neighborhood, their turf.

This is exactly what makes **на районе** feel more like **"in the hood"** than just "in the neighborhood."

What "на районе" Means Culturally

In Russian youth and street culture, especially in hip-hop and rap, **на районе** refers to more than just a physical place. It's:

A **tight-knit local world** where people grow up, hustle, and survive

A place that can be **tough, poor, or gritty**, but where there's also pride, loyalty, and community

A way of saying: "This is where I come from... and I'm proud of it, no matter what"

This subculture has its own slang, values, and unwritten rules. Much like "the block" in American hip-hop, **на районе** represents the environment that shapes people and gives them something to fight for or rise above.

So when the title says **Жизнь на районе**, it's not just talking about geography; it's a whole worldview. The song gives voice to that experience: life in the hood, with its **struggles, rules, ambition, and pride**.

First Listening

Before doing anything else, just listen to the song from beginning to end. Don't read the lyrics yet. Just focus on what you can pick up by ear.

Ask yourself:

- What kind of mood or energy does the song have?
- Are there any words or phrases you recognize?
- Can you tell what the song is about, even a little?

You don't need to understand everything right away. This step is just about getting a first impression.

Key Words

Every song has a core set of words and phrases that carry its meaning, tone, and emotional weight. In Жизнь на райóне, many of the key words come from **slang, everyday speech, and motivational language**, giving the lyrics a raw, real-world feel.

This song is about **survival, hustle, ambition, and loyalty.** The vocabulary reflects that, blending street slang with deeper expressions of independence and resilience.

Second Listening: Listen for These Words

As you listen to the song **for the second time**, focus on picking out the following words **in the forms they appear in the lyrics.** You may already understand some of them, or they might be new to you. Either way, just **try to catch them by ear** and **check the box** when you hear them.

☐ на райóне   ☐ бúтва

☐ пацаны́   ☐ вы́зов

☐ крутúть   ☐ квадрáт

☐ тáчках   ☐ прáвила

☐ пáчках   ☐ цель

These words appear in important lines or are repeated themes in the song. Listen for how they're used, and notice how they contribute to the overall message.

Slang vs. Standard Vocabulary

Many of the key words in this song come from **urban slang and informal Russian**. These words help create the song's tone: gritty, real, and full of attitude. Others are standard Russian words you might hear in school or formal writing.

Knowing which is which helps you understand both **how people actually speak** and **when different words are appropriate**.

Slang or Colloquial Words

- **на райо́не** – Slang phrase. Nonstandard grammar ("в районе" is correct), but **на районе** is widely used in youth and urban slang to mean "in the hood."
- **пацаны́** – Slang. Means "guys" or "bros"; more informal than парни or ребята.
- **крути́ть** – Slang when used in this context. Literally means "to spin," but here it means "to hustle" or "to be in the game."
- **та́чках** – Slang. From **тачка**, meaning "car" (like "ride" in English).
- **па́чках** – Slang. **Пачка** means "pack" (like of cigarettes or bills), but in slang it refers to **stacks of cash**.
- **квадра́т** – Colloquial. Literally "square," but used here to mean a "block" or area of territory.

Standard or Neutral Words

- **би́тва** – Standard. Means "battle."
- **вы́зов** – Standard. "Challenge" or "call."
- **пра́вила** – Standard. "Rules."
- **цель** – Standard. "Goal" or "target."

First Look at the Lyrics

Before we go line by line in the Breakdown section, take some time to get familiar with the lyrics and see what you can figure out on your own. You don't need to understand everything just yet. This step is about getting a feel for the song, spotting key words, and making your own observations first.

Step 1: Listen and Read Along

Turn to the full lyrics on page 55.

- Play the song and **follow along with the Russian text** as you listen.
- Let the words flow. You don't need to stop or translate anything yet.

Step 2: Read Without the Music

Now go back and read through the lyrics **slowly on your own**, without the song playing.

- Take your time with each line.
- Try to **find the 10 key words** from the previous section as you go.
- When you see one, **underline it** and try to guess what the line might mean based on context.

You don't need to get it exactly right. Just make your best guess. You're training your reading and inference skills.

Step 3: Compare with the English Translation

Now turn to the English translation (page 56) and compare it to the Russian.

- See how close your guesses were.
- Pay attention to how the **key words** are used in context.
- Notice anything surprising or different from how you expected the line to work.

Step 4: Listen Again

- Listen to the song one more time. This time with a **new understanding** of what's being said.
- You might find that you catch more, understand more, and feel more connected to the rhythm and message of the lyrics.

You're now ready for the full breakdown.

Breakdown

Now let's look closely at how the Russian works, one line at a time.

In this section, we'll look at:

- Key vocabulary and phrases
- Grammar points (verb tense, noun cases, etc.)
- How the lines are structured and why they work in Russian

На райо́не пацаны́ зна́ют, как жить

- **на райо́не** – in the hood (slang; grammatically it would be "в райо́не")
- **пацаны́** – guys, bros (slang for ребя́та or па́рни)
- **зна́ют** – they know (3rd person plural of знать)
- **как жить** – how to live (infinitive verb phrase)

День за днём — бе́гать, крути́ть, не спать, не тупи́ть

- **день за днём** – day by day (fixed phrase)
- **бе́гать** – to run (imperfective infinitive)
- **крути́ть** – to hustle (slang; literally "to spin")
- **не спать** – not to sleep
- **не тупи́ть** – don't slow down (slang; тупи́ть = to act slow, dull)

Кто́-то в спо́ртзале, кто́-то на та́чках

- **кто́-то** – someone (indefinite pronoun)
- **в спо́ртзале** – in the gym (prepositional case)
- **на та́чках** – in cars (slang; та́чка = car)

Кто́-то мечта́ет подня́ться на па́чках

- **мечта́ет** – dreams (3rd person singular of мечта́ть)
- **подня́ться** – to rise, to make it (perfective infinitive)
- **на па́чках** – on stacks (slang; па́чка = stack, here of money)

Chorus

Жизнь на райо́не — э́то би́тва

- **жизнь** – life (feminine noun)
- **на райо́не** – in the hood (slang)

- **это битва** – it's a battle (feminine noun)

Ка́ждый день но́вый вы́зов, брат

- **каждый день** – every day
- **новый вызов** – new challenge (masculine adjective + noun)
- **брат** – bro (informal address)

Но я иду́ то́лько вы́ше

- **я иду** – I go / I walk (1st person singular of идти)
- **только выше** – only higher (comparative of высокий)

Зна́ю: сам за себя́, сам за свой квадра́т

- **знаю** – I know (1st person singular)
- **сам за себя** – by myself / for myself (reflexive, idiomatic expression)
- **сам за свой квадрат** – for my block (slang; квадрат = square, here "territory")

Verse 2

Магази́н у до́ма — ме́сто встреч

- **магазин у дома** – the store by the house
- **место встреч** – meeting place (genitive plural of встреча)

Двор — э́то шко́ла, где у́чат мечта́ть и жечь

- **двор** – courtyard / yard (masculine noun)
- **это школа** – is a school (это is used in place of "is" in these kinds of identifying sentences. It's not a verb, but it does the job of connecting the subject and the complement when a linking word is needed.)
- **где учат** – where they teach
- **мечтать** – to dream (infinitive)

- **жечь** – to burn (metaphorically: to shine, live intensely)

Здесь свои пра́вила, свои геро́и

- **здесь** – here
- **свои правила** – our own rules
- **свои герои** – our own heroes (possessive adjective agrees with plural nouns)

Вре́мя пока́жет, кто ста́нет каки́м в э́том стро́е

- **время покажет** – time will show (future tense)
- **кто станет** – who will become (future tense of стать)
- **каким** – what kind / how (instrumental case)
- **в этом строе** – in this system / structure (prepositional case of строй)

Бридж

Нет ничего́, что даётся легко́

- **нет ничего** – there's nothing
- **что даётся легко** – that comes easily / is given easily (passive construction of давать)

Путь непросто́й, но я зна́ю одно́

- **путь** – path (masculine noun)
- **непростой** – not easy (adjective)
- **но я знаю одно** – but I know one thing

Е́сли есть цель — ты до́лжен идти́

- **если есть цель** – if there is a goal
- **должен идти** – must go (modal verb + infinitive)

Жизнь прове́рит, смо́жешь ли ты

- **жизнь проверит** – life will test

- **сможешь ли ты** – whether you can (future tense of **смочь** + question particle **ли**)

Lyrics

Куплéт 1

На райóне пацаны́ зна́ют, как жить,

День за днём — бéгать, крути́ть, не спать, не тупи́ть.

Ктó-то в спортза́ле, ктó-то на та́чках,

Ктó-то мечта́ет подня́ться на па́чках.

припéв

Жизнь на райóне — э́то би́тва,

Ка́ждый день нóвый вы́зов, брат.

Но я иду́ тóлько вы́ше,

Зна́ю: сам за себя́, сам за свой квадра́т.

Куплéт 2

Магази́н у дóма — мéсто встреч,

Двор — э́то шкóла, где у́чат мечта́ть и жечь.

Здесь свой пра́вила, свой герóи,

Врéмя пока́жет, кто ста́нет каки́м в э́том стрóе.

(Припéв)

Бридж

Нет ничегó, что даётся легкó,

Путь непростóй, но я зна́ю однó:

Éсли есть цель — ты дóлжен идти́,

Жизнь провéрит, смóжешь ли ты.

(Припéв)

Translation

Verse 1

In the hood, the guys know how to live,

Day by day... run, hustle, no sleep, no slip.

Some are in the gym, some flex their cars,

Some dream of rising up off cash stacks.

Chorus

Life in the hood, it's a battle,

Every day a new challenge, bro.

But I'm only going higher,

I know: I stand for myself, for my block.

Verse 2

The shop by the house... the meetup spot,

The yard is a school where dreams burn hot.

Here we've got our own rules, our own heroes,

Time will tell who stands where in this row.

(Chorus)

Bridge

Nothing in life comes easy,

The road is tough, but I know one thing:

If you have a goal, you have to go,

Life will test if you can hold.

(Chorus)

Song Title

The title **Сильне́е всех** means **"Stronger Than All."** It's short, bold, and grammatically rich.

Let's break it down:

- **си́льный** – strong (adjective, masculine)
- **сильне́е** – stronger (comparative form)
- **всех** – than all (genitive plural of **все** – everyone)

In Russian, comparisons are often made using the **comparative form of the adjective** followed by the noun in the **genitive case**. So:

сильне́е всех = stronger than all (others)

This structure is very common in Russian and packs a lot of meaning into just two words. It expresses not just strength, but **superiority**, **self-belief**, and **pride**, all major themes of the song.

First Listening

Before you look at the lyrics, listen to the song once all the way through.

You don't need to understand everything yet. Just get a sense of:

- The energy and emotion of the song
- Any words or phrases that stand out to you
- What kind of message the singer is trying to send

This first impression will help you connect more deeply when we explore the lyrics in detail.

Key Words

'I Am' Statements

All of these phrases are in the **first person singular**, "I" statements. Since the singer is female, some forms reflect **feminine agreement**, especially in past tense or with short-form adjectives. We'll also show you how a **man would say it**, when it would be different.

☐ **Я сильнее́е всех** – I am stronger than all (Uses the comparative adjective сильне́е.)

☐ **Я не бою́сь** – I'm not afraid

☐ **Я встаю́ и иду́** – I get up and go

☐ **Я зна́ю, что всё по плечу́** – I know I can handle it all (по плечу́ = "within my ability"; fixed expression.)

☐ **Я разруша́ю сте́ну** – I break the wall

☐ **Я никогда́ не сда́мся** – I will never give up (Reflexive verb in future tense)

☐ **Я вы́ше небе́с** – I am higher than the skies

☐ **Я не одна́** – I'm not alone (feminine) (A man would say: **Я не один**)

☐ **Я поднимусь́** – I will rise (Future tense, reflexive)

☐ **Я рожде́на, чтоб свети́ть** – I was born to shine (feminine short-form adjective) (A man would say: **Я рожден, чтоб свети́ть**)

These kinds of sentences are great for practicing how to express **who you are** in Russian, confidently and naturally. After listening, try to say a few of them yourself, or even write your own "I am..." line using one of the key words.

Second Listening

Now listen to the song again, but this time, **join in**.

As you hear the "I am" statements from the list above, **sing them out loud** with the singer. Try to **match her rhythm, pronunciation, and confidence**. This technique is called **shadowing**, and it's a great way to improve your speaking and fluency.

Don't worry about being perfect. Just go for it. Own it!

First Look at the Lyrics

Before we break down the lyrics line by line, take a few minutes to explore the song on your own. This step helps you build listening and reading skills while giving you a chance to connect with the song personally.

Step 1: Listen and Read Along

Turn to the full Russian lyrics (page 66).
Play the song and follow along with the words as you listen. Don't pause or try to translate. Just focus on the **sound** and **flow** of the language.

Step 2: Read Without the Music

Now read the lyrics again, slowly and without the audio.

- Underline or highlight words you recognize.
- Look out for the **"I am" statements** from the Key Words section.

- Try to guess the meaning of the lines that contain them.

Reading without the music gives you more time to notice details: word endings, repeated phrases, and how the lines are structured.

Step 3: Compare with the English Translation

Turn to the English translation (page 67) and go line by line.

- See how close your guesses were.
- Take note of **new words or useful expressions**.
- Notice any **differences in how things are phrased** in Russian versus English.

Step 4: Listen Again

Play the song one more time, now with a deeper understanding of what's being said.

This is a good time to **sing or speak along**, using the lyrics to help with pronunciation and flow. Let the language and energy sink in!

Breakdown

Let's take a closer look at the lyrics line by line. This song is packed with bold verbs, poetic expressions, and personal declarations of strength. We'll unpack:

- Useful vocabulary and expressions
- Key grammar points (cases, verb forms, comparatives, etc.)
- How the lines are built and why they work in Russian

Смотрю́ в зе́ркало – ви́жу си́лу в глаза́х

- **смотрю** – I look (1st person singular, present)
- **в зеркало** – in the mirror (accusative case of зеркало, neuter noun)
- **вижу** – I see (1st person singular, present)
- **силу** – strength (accusative case of сила, feminine noun)
- **в глазах** – in (my) eyes (prepositional plural of глаз)

Я не бою́сь, ведь мой страх — в пустяка́х

- **не бою́сь** – I'm not afraid (reflexive verb бояться, 1st person singular)
- **ведь** – because / after all
- **мой страх** – my fear (nominative)
- **в пустяках** – in little things (prepositional plural of пустяк – trivial thing)

Е́сли упа́ла – встаю́ и иду́

- **если** – if
- **упала** – (I) fell (past tense, feminine form of упасть)
- **встаю** – I get up (1st person singular, present of вставать)
- **иду** – I go (1st person singular, present of идти)

Я зна́ю, что всё по плечу́!

- **знаю** – I know (1st person singular, present)
- **что всё по плечу** – that I can handle it all
- **по плечу** – literally "on the shoulder," but idiomatically means "manageable" or "within one's strength"

Ты говори́шь, что я не смогу́

- **говоришь** – you say (2nd person singular, present)
- **что я не смогу** – that I won't be able to (future tense of мочь)

Но знай, я разруша́ю сте́ну!

- **знай** – know! (imperative of знать)
- **разрушаю** – I destroy (1st person singular, present)
- **стену** – wall (accusative of стена, feminine noun)

Сме́ло шагну́ навстре́чу мечте́

- **смело** – bravely, boldly (adverb)
- **шагну** – I will step (future of шагнуть, perfective)
- **навстречу** – toward (preposition, requires dative case)
- **мечте** – to (my) dream (dative case of мечта)

Я никогда́ не сда́мся!

- **никогда́ не сда́мся** – I will never give up
- **сда́мся** – future tense of сдаваться (reflexive verb, 1st person)

Chorus

Я сильне́е всех, я вы́ше небе́с

- **сильнее всех** – stronger than all (comparative adjective + genitive plural)
- **выше небес** – higher than the skies (comparative adjective + genitive plural of небо)

Мир откро́ется мне, е́сли ве́рю в успе́х

- **мир** – the world

- **откроется мне** – will open to me (future, reflexive of **откры́ться**)
- **ве́рю в успе́х** – I believe in success
    - **в успе́х** – accusative case (after **в**)
    - **верю** – 1st person present of верить

Не останови́ть, не сбить мне полёт

- **не остановить** – (it) can't be stopped (impersonal construction, infinitive)
- **не сбить мне полёт** – (they) can't knock down my flight
    - **сбить** – to knock down
    - **мне** – dative case (shows who's affected)
    - **полёт** – flight (masculine, accusative)

Я лечу́ то́лько вперёд!

- **лечу** – I fly (1st person present of лететь)
- **только вперёд** – only forward

Verse 2

Девчо́нка с хара́ктером – э́то про меня́

- **девчонка** – girl (colloquial form of девушка)
- **с характером** – with character (instrumental case)
- **это про меня** – that's about me (про + accusative)

Я зна́ю, что я не одна́!

- **не одна** – not alone (feminine form; A man would say: Я не один)

Сёстры мои́ – сме́лость и свет

- **сёстры** – sisters
- **мои** – my (plural)
- **смелость и свет** – courage and light

Вме́сте сильне́е – нас не слома́ть, нет!

- **вместе сильнее** – stronger together (comparative)
- **нас не слома́ть** – we can't be broken (impersonal, **сломать** = to break, infinitive)

Bridge

Ско́лько бы раз ни пыта́лись слома́ть

- **сколько бы раз** – however many times
- **ни пытались** – they tried (past tense, plural + concessive **ни**)
- **сломать** – to break (infinitive)

Я подниму́сь – меня́ не ну́жно спаса́ть!

- **поднимусь** – I will rise (future tense, 1st person singular of **подняться**, reflexive)
- **меня не нужно спасать** – I don't need saving
  - **меня** – me (accusative case)
  - **не нужно** – it's not necessary (impersonal)
  - **спасать** – to save/rescue (imperfective infinitive)

Why is it "меня́" and not "мне"?
You might expect **мне** here because you've probably learned phrases like **"мне ну́жно"** to mean "I need…" But in this line, the structure is different.

The phrase **"не ну́жно спаса́ть"** is an **impersonal construction** that means "it's not necessary to save…", and the verb **спаса́ть** (to save) is **transitive**. That means it needs a **direct object** (the person being saved) in the **accusative case**.

So you're not saying "I need to save," or "I need saving," but: "It's not necessary to save me."

Свет во мне гори́т, не потуши́ть

- **свет во мне горит** – the light in me burns
- **не потушить** – can't be put out (impersonal infinitive construction)

Я рожде́на, чтоб свети́ть!

- **рождена** – I was born (short-form passive participle, feminine; A man would say: Я рожден)
- **чтоб светить** – to shine (infinitive; contraction of чтобы)

Lyrics

Куплéт 1

Смотрю́ в зéркало – ви́жу си́лу в глазáх,

Я не бою́сь, ведь мой страх — в пустякáх.

Éсли упáла – встаю́ и иду́,

Я знáю, что всё по плечу́!

предприпéв

Ты говори́шь, что я не смогу́,

Но знай, я разрушáю стéну!

Смéло шагну́ навстрéчу мечтé –

Я никогдá не сдáмся!

припéв

Я сильнéе всех, я вы́ше небéс,

Мир открóется мне, éсли вéрю в успéх!

Не останови́ть, не сбить мне полёт,

Я лечу́ тóлько вперёд!

Куплéт 2

Девчóнка с харáктером – э́то про меня́,

Я знáю, что я не однá!

Сёстры мои́ – смéлость и свет,

Вмéсте сильнéе – нас не сломáть, нет!

(Предприпéв + Припéв)

Бридж

Скóлько бы раз ни пытáлись сломáть,

Я поднимỳсь – меня́ не нỳжно спасáть!

Свет во мне гори́т, не потуши́ть,

Я рождена́, чтоб свети́ть!   (Припéв)

Translation

Verse 1

I look in the mirror – I see strength in my eyes,

I'm not afraid, my fear is in little things.

If I fall down, I get up and go,

I know that I can handle it all!

Pre-Chorus

You say that I won't succeed,

But know that I will break the wall!

I take a bold step toward my dream –

I will never give up!

Chorus

I'm stronger than all, I'm higher than the sky,

The world will open to me if I believe in success!

You can't stop me, you can't knock me down,

I am flying only forward!

Verse 2

A girl with character – that's who I am,

I know that I'm not alone!

My sisters are courage and light,

Together we're stronger – we can't be broken, no!

(Pre-Chorus + Chorus)

Bridge

No matter how many times they try to break me,

I will rise – I don't need saving!

The light in me burns, it won't go out,

I was born to shine! (Chorus)

Song_Title_

The title **Ох уж э́тот ру́сский!** translates to **"Oh, This Russian!"** – a phrase that perfectly captures the frustration every Russian learner knows all too well. You've probably cursed the seemingly unnecessarily complicated grammar: the verb conjugations, the use of cases, the countless irregularities, and of course, the ever-shifting stress. This song embraces that struggle with humor, honesty, and a whole lot of determination.

Let's break it down:

- **Ох** – an exclamation, like "Oh!" or "Ugh!" depending on tone.
- **уж** – a little filler word that adds emphasis, hard to translate directly, but it reinforces frustration or intensity.
- **этот русский** – this Russian (meaning the language, not a person).

So the full phrase has a tone of **playful exasperation**. The singer is clearly struggling, but he's still in the game!

Russian can feel like a wild puzzle: **stress that moves**, **verbs with pairs**, **cases that change everything**, and words that seem impossible to pronounce. This song taps into that feeling: the confusion, the mistakes, the "Wait... why is it лю́ди and not челове́ки?" moments.

First Listening

Before you look at the lyrics, just press play and listen to the song from start to finish.

- Don't worry about understanding every word. Just focus on the sound, the rhythm, and anything familiar that jumps out.
- Do you recognize any grammar terms? Case names? Verbs you've studied?

This first listen is all about getting a feel for the song. We'll take it apart step by step right after.

Key Words

Did They Really Say That?

This song perfectly captures the ups and downs of learning Russian: the confusing rules, the strange exceptions, the stress that never lands where you expect it to. Instead of just listing vocabulary, let's have some fun with it.

Below are some of the most confusing or frustrating grammar-related moments from the song. For each one, see if you can choose the correct answer based on what the singer says... or what you already know!

No pressure. Just see what you recognize, and maybe laugh along the way.

As you listen to the song again, pay special attention to these confusing grammar terms and phrases. You'll find them all in the lyrics. Afterward, try the quiz below.

Mini-Quiz: What's the Confusion?

1. The **teacher** says звони́т, but the singer's **friend** says:

A) зво́нит

B) сфо́нит

C) звони́д

2. What's the deal with **лю́ди** and **челове́ки**?

A) Both are correct but used differently

B) One is singular, the other plural

C) Both mean "people," but only **лю́ди** is grammatically correct

3. What's confusing about **соверше́нный / несоверше́нный**?

A) They are two of the six (or is it seven?) grammatical cases

B) They're verb aspects: completed vs. ongoing

C) They mean "regular" and "irregular"

4. The line mentions **да́тельный** and **твори́тельный**. What are those?

A) Regional dialects of Russian

B) Two of the six (or is it seven?) grammatical cases

C) Styles of handwriting

5. The phrase **по́лный тупи́к** means:

A) A complete stop

B) A dead end

C) A grammar term you forgot again

6. When the singer says **почти́ без оши́бок**, she means:

A) He gave up on Russian

B) He's learned to live with the mistakes

C) He's finally speaking almost without errors

Answer Key + Explanations

1. A) звÓнит

The correct pronunciation is **звонИ́т** (stress on the last syllable), but many native speakers say **звÓнит**, which drives teachers (and learners!) crazy. The song reflects this real-life confusion.

2. C) Both mean "people," but only лю́ди is grammatically correct

You might think the plural of челове́к (person) would be челове́ки, but nope! The correct plural is лю́ди, a completely different word. This irregularity stumps almost everyone.

3. B) They're verb aspects: completed vs. ongoing

Соверше́нный means "perfective" (a completed action), and несоверше́нный means "imperfective" (ongoing or repeated action). These aspects are a major challenge for Russian learners, especially when the difference doesn't exist in your native language.

4. B) Two of the six (or is it seven?) grammatical cases

Да́тельный is the **dative case** (used to indicate the recipient of an action), and твори́тельный is the **instrumental case** (used to show what something is done with). Learners often confuse them or forget what they're for entirely. These cases answer: кому? (to whom?) and чем? (with what?)

5. B) A dead end

The phrase по́лный тупи́к literally means "a complete dead end." In the song, it refers to being totally stuck or lost in grammar, something every learner has felt at least once (okay, many times).

6. C) He's finally speaking almost without errors

Почти без ошибок = almost without mistakes. It's a moment of triumph. The singer finally feels like he's getting the hang of it. A proud (and rare!) moment for any learner.

First Look at the Lyrics

Before we start breaking down the lines, let's take a few minutes to explore the lyrics on your own. This step helps you build confidence and spot patterns, even before we explain them.

Step 1: Listen and Read Along

Turn to the Russian lyrics on page 77.

Play the song and follow along with the text as you listen. Don't stop or overthink it. Just try to get a feel for the rhythm, pronunciation, and any words or phrases you recognize.

Step 2: Read Without the Music

Now go back and read the lyrics **slowly**, without the audio.

- Look for grammar words and terms that come up (like падежи or совершённый).
- Can you spot any of the confusing examples mentioned in the chorus or bridge?
- Try to guess what the singer is frustrated about, even if you don't know every word.

Step 3: Compare with the English Translation

Flip to the English translation (page 78) and go line by line.

- See how close your guesses were.
- Notice how Russian expresses frustration, confusion, or determination differently than English.
- Circle any new words you want to learn or use yourself.

Step 4: Listen Again

Now that you know what the lyrics mean, listen to the song one more time.

You might catch more words this time or finally hear what used to sound like a blur. Bonus: try mouthing or singing along with the grammar words for extra practice.

Breakdown

Let's go line by line to explore the grammar, vocabulary, and structure behind this fun and all-too-relatable song. We'll point out useful expressions, case usage, verb forms, and the grammar terms that every Russian learner has wrestled with.

Verse 1

Я учу́ ру́сский, но как нелегко́!

- **учу** – I learn / I'm learning (present tense, 1st person singular of учить)
- **русский** – Russian (adjective, short for русский язык)
- **но как нелегко!** – but how difficult it is!
    - **как** – how (expresses intensity)
    - **нелегко** – not easy (adverb from лёгкий, "easy")

Где ударе́ние? Сно́ва не то!

- **ударение** – stress (neuter noun; in pronunciation)
- **снова не то** – again it's wrong
- **не то** – not the right one / not correct

Друг сказа́л «зво́нит», а учи́тель – «звони́т»

- **друг сказал** – a friend said (past tense, masculine)
- **учитель – «звони́т»** – the teacher says "zvonít" (correct stress)

This line plays on the common confusion about where to place stress in Russian words, especially **звонить**.

Как же пра́вильно мне говори́ть?

- **как же** – but how / how on earth (adds emphasis)
- **правильно** – correctly (adverb)
- **мне говорить** – for me to speak (dative + infinitive)

Chorus

Ох уж э́тот ру́сский – сло́жный язы́к!

- **ох уж этот** – oh, this [annoying] one! (adds humorous frustration)
- **русский** – Russian
- **сложный язык** – a difficult language
  - **сложный** – complicated/difficult
  - **язык** – language (masculine noun)

Склоне́ния, спряже́ния – по́лный тупи́к!

- **склонения** – declensions (noun/adjective endings that change by case)
- **спряжения** – conjugations (verb endings that change by person/tense)

- **полный тупик** – total dead end (idiom for feeling completely lost)

Но я не сда́мся, я бу́ду учи́ть

- **не сдамся** – I won't give up (future tense of сдаваться, reflexive)
- **буду учить** – I will study (future construction with буду + infinitive)

Когда́-нибу́дь бу́ду свобо́дно говори́ть!

- **когда-нибудь** – someday / eventually
- **свободно говорить** – speak fluently (literally "freely")

Verse 2

Два бра́та, но три стола́ – как поня́ть?

- **два брата** – two brothers (note: брат has irregular plural forms)
- **три стола** – three tables (plural of стол)
- **как понять?** – how to understand? (infinitive construction)

А почему́ лю́ди, но не челове́ки опя́ть?

- **люди** – people (correct, irregular plural of человек)
- **человеки** – incorrect plural (included for humor; it's a common learner mistake)
- **опять?** – again?

Соверше́нный? Несоверше́нный?

- Refers to verb aspects:
  - **совершенный** – perfective (completed action)
  - **несовершенный** – imperfective (ongoing/repeated action)

И вот я совершённо растёрянный!

- **и вот я...** – and now I... (signals sudden realization)
- **совершенно** – completely (adverb)
- **растерянный** – confused / bewildered (past passive participle)

Дáтельный, творúтельный – что áто знáчит?

- **дательный** – dative case (used to indicate the recipient)
- **творительный** – instrumental case (used to indicate the means or tool)
- **что это значит?** – what does this mean?

Я пýтаю падежú и словá не звучáт!

- **путаю падежи** – I mix up the cases
- **слова не звучат** – the words don't sound right
    - **звучат** – they sound (3rd person plural)

Но вдруг я пóнял – мне стáло легкó

- **вдруг** – suddenly
- **понял** – understood (past tense, masculine of понять)
- **мне стáло легко** – it became easy for me
    - **мне** – dative case
    - **легко** – easy (adverb)

Тепéрь я говорю́ почтú без ошúбок!

- **теперь** – now
- **говорю** – I speak
- **почти без ошúбок** – almost without mistakes
    - **ошибок** – genitive plural of ошибка (mistake)

Lyrics

Куплет 1

Я учу́ ру́сский, но как нелегко́!

Где ударе́ние? Сно́ва не то!

Друг сказа́л «звО́нит», а учи́тель – «звонИ́т»,

Как же пра́вильно мне говори́ть?

припев

Ох уж э́тот ру́сский – сло́жный язы́к!

Склоне́ния, спряже́ния – по́лный тупи́к!

Но я не сда́мся, я бу́ду учи́ть,

Когда́-нибу́дь бу́ду свобо́дно говори́ть!

Куплет 2

Два бра́та, но три стола́ – как поня́ть?

А почему́ лю́ди, но не челове́ки опя́ть?

Соверше́нный? Несоверше́нный?

И вот я соверше́нно расте́рянный!

(Припе́в)

Бридж

Да́тельный, твори́тельный – что э́то зна́чит?

Я пу́таю падежи́ и слова́ не звуча́т!

Но вдруг я по́нял – мне ста́ло легко́,

Тепе́рь я говорю́ почти́ без оши́бок!

(Припе́в)

Translation

Verse 1

I'm learning Russian, but it's so hard!

Where is the stress? Again, it's wrong!

A friend said "zvOnit", but my teacher – "zvonIt",

How should I say it right?

Chorus

Oh, this Russian – such a tough language!

Declensions, conjugations – a total mess!

But I won't give up, I will keep learning,

Someday I'll speak fluently!

Verse 2

Two brothers, but three tables – how to understand?

And why lyudi but never cheloveki again?

Perfective? Imperfective?

And now I'm completely confused!

(Chorus)

Bridge

Dative, instrumental – what does that mean?

I mix up the cases, and words don't sound right!

But suddenly, I got it – it became easy,

Now I speak almost without mistakes!

(Chorus)

Song Title

The title **Ночь для нас** means **"A Night for Us."** Simple, right? But it's also a great reminder of how Russian handles pronouns after prepositions, something learners often forget.

Let's break it down:

- **ночь** – night (feminine noun, in the nominative case here)
- **для** – for (a preposition that always takes the **genitive case**)
- **нас** – us (genitive form of мы)

So even though "we" in Russian is мы, after для it becomes нас. It's a completely different form (and one that often trips learners up), but it's used **all the time** in natural Russian.

Here's a quick refresher on **personal pronouns in the genitive case** (used after prepositions like для, у, без, от, etc.):

Pronoun	Nominative	Genitive
I	я	меня
you (sing.)	ты	тебя
he	он	него
she	она	неё
we	мы	нас
you (pl.)	вы	вас
they	они	них

Also, take a look at the **third-person pronouns** in the chart above. You'll notice an extra "н-" at the beginning: него, неё, них. This **"н-" only appears after prepositions**.

If the genitive form is used **without a preposition**, that н- disappears:

- **Ты бои́шься его́?** – Are you afraid of him?
  (no preposition, so no н-)
- **Без него́ ску́чно.** – Without him, it's boring.
  (preposition → add н-)
- **У неё нет кни́ги.** – She doesn't have the book.
  (preposition → add н-)

First Listening

Listen to the song from beginning to end without reading the lyrics yet.
Try to absorb the **atmosphere** of the night. Can you catch any familiar words about light, time, movement, or feelings?

You're not expected to understand everything yet. Just enjoy the sound of the language and the vibe of the song. We'll take it step by step from here.

Key Words

Light, Sound, and Movement

Some songs tell a story with events. This one paints a **feeling**. The lyrics are full of words that create a dreamy, glowing night full of music, laughter, and motion. These words may not be hard on their own, but they appear in poetic forms that can be tricky to catch when sung.

Below are 10 important words taken directly from the song lyrics. As you listen, try to catch them. They're not just vocabulary; they're the mood of the night.

Listen to the song again. Don't worry about understanding every line. Just try to **catch these 10 words** and check them off as you hear them.

☐ све́тит	☐ запо́мним
☐ лу́нный	☐ кру́жится
☐ смеёмся	☐ гори́т
☐ шага́ем	☐ танцу́ем
☐ живёт	☐ улыба́емся

Even if you only catch a few this time, that's progress! You'll see all of these again as we break the lyrics down together.

First Look at the Lyrics

Before we break things down line by line, take a few minutes to explore the lyrics on your own. This is your chance to train your eyes and ears before we explain anything in detail.

Step 1: Read While Listening

Turn to the Russian lyrics on page 87 and play the song.

Follow along with the text as you listen. Don't worry about understanding everything. Just get familiar with the sound and flow.

Step 2: Find the Key Words

As you read and listen, look for the **10 key words** from the last section. Can you spot them in the lyrics? Circle or underline them.

Now, without using a dictionary, try to **guess the meaning of each word** based on the sentence it appears in.

What kind of atmosphere or action is being described? What do you feel the word must mean?

Step 3: Check the English Translation

Flip to the English lyrics (page 89) and compare what you guessed to the actual translation.

Did you get close? Did some meanings surprise you?

This step helps build your confidence in **reading in context**, a powerful skill for language learning.

Breakdown

Verse 1

Звёзды я́рко све́тят в не́бе

- **звёзды** – stars (plural, nominative)
- **я́рко** – brightly (adverb)
- **све́тят** – shine (3rd person plural, present tense of светить)
- **в не́бе** – in the sky (prepositional case of небо)

Ве́тер тёплый нас зовёт

- **ветер** – wind (masculine noun, nominative)
- **тёплый** – warm (adjective, nominative, masculine, agrees with ветер)
- **нас** – us (accusative form of мы)
- **зовёт** – calls (3rd person singular, present of звать)

Снóва ýлицы так светлы́

- **снова** – again
- **улицы** – streets (plural, nominative)
- **так** – so (intensifier)
- **светлы** – bright (short-form plural adjective of светлый)

Гóрод вéсело живёт

- **город** – city (masculine noun, nominative)
- **весело** – cheerfully, joyfully (adverb)
- **живёт** – lives (3rd person singular, present of жить)

Pre-Chorus

Мы шагáем, мы смеёмся

- **шагаем** – we walk (1st person plural, present of шагать)
- **смеёмся** – we laugh (1st person plural, present of смеяться, reflexive)

Э́та ночь для нас гори́т

- **эта ночь** – this night (feminine noun, nominative)
- **для нас** – for us (нас is genitive form of мы, used after для)
- **горит** – burns (3rd person singular, present of гореть) – here, metaphorical: the night is glowing/alive

Мýзыка вокрýг смеётся

- **музыка** – music (feminine noun, nominative)
- **вокруг** – around
- **смеётся** – laughs (3rd person singular, present of смеяться) – personification

Всё кру́жится и блести́т!

- **всё** – everything (neuter, nominative)
- **кружится** – spins/twirls (3rd person singular, present, reflexive of крутить)
- **блестит** – shines/sparkles (3rd person singular, present of блестеть)

Chorus

Эй, подру́ги, вре́мя вы́шло

- **Эй** – Hey
- **подруги** – girlfriends, female friends (nominative plural of подруга)
- **время вышло** – time is up
    - **вышло** – came out, ran out (past tense, neuter, perfective of выйти)

Ско́ро бу́дет но́вый день!

- **скоро** – soon
- **будет** – will be (3rd person singular future of быть)
- **новый день** – a new day (masculine, nominative)

Но пока́ что мы танцу́ем

- **пока что** – for now
- **танцуем** – we are dancing (1st person plural, present of танцевать)

Пусть нам све́тит лу́нный свет

- **пусть** – let (used to express hope/wish)
- **нам** – to us (dative case of мы)
- **светит** – shines (present tense of светить)

- **лу́нный свет** – moonlight (masculine noun phrase; literally "moonlight shines to us")

Verse 2

Не́бо в я́рких огонька́х

- **не́бо** – sky (neuter, nominative)
- **в ярких огоньках** – in bright lights (prepositional plural; **огонёк** = little light, flame)

Го́лос у́лиц — э́то ритм

- **голос** – voice (masculine, nominative)
- **улиц** – of the streets (genitive plural of улица)
- **это ритм** – it's rhythm / this is rhythm

Мы запо́мним э́тот ве́чер

- **запомним** – we will remember (future, perfective of запомнить)
- **этот вечер** – this evening (masculine, accusative)

Сло́вно сла́дкий, тёплый стих

- **словно** – like, as if
- **сладкий, тёплый** – sweet, warm (masculine adjectives)
- **стих** – poem (masculine noun)

Bridge

Вре́мя бы́стро убега́ет

- **вре́мя** – time
- **бы́стро** – quickly (adverb)
- **убега́ет** – is running away (present tense of убегать)

Но в душе́ ого́нь живёт

- **в душе** – in the soul (prepositional of душа, feminine noun)
- **огонь** – fire (masculine noun)
- **живёт** – lives (3rd person singular, present of жить)

Э́та ночь нас окрыля́ет

- **окрыля́ет** – inspires, lifts up (present of окрылять, from крыло = wing)

Пусть она́ не пропадёт!

- **не пропадёт** – let it not fade away / disappear (future, perfective of пропадать)

Outro

Эй, подру́ги, не проща́емся

- **не прощаемся** – we are not saying goodbye (reflexive, imperfective, 1st person plural of прощаться)

Пусть запо́мнится моме́нт!

- **запомнится** – will be remembered (perfective, reflexive future of запомниться)
- **момент** – moment (masculine noun)

Мы танцу́ем, улыба́емся

- **улыбаемся** – we are smiling (1st person plural, reflexive of улыбаться)

Lyrics

Куплёт 1

Звёзды я́рко све́тят в не́бе,

Ве́тер тёплый нас зовёт.

Сно́ва у́лицы так светлы́,

Го́род ве́село живёт.

предприпе́в

Мы шага́ем, мы смеёмся,

Э́та ночь для нас гори́т.

Му́зыка вокру́г смеётся,

Всё кру́жится и блести́т!

припе́в

Эй, подру́ги, вре́мя вы́шло,

Ско́ро бу́дет но́вый день!

Но пока́ что мы танцу́ем,

Пусть нам све́тит лу́нный свет.

Куплёт 2

Не́бо в я́рких огонька́х,

Го́лос у́лиц — э́то ритм.

Мы запо́мним э́тот ве́чер,

Сло́вно сла́дкий, тёплый стих.

(Предприпе́в + Припе́в)

Бридж

Вре́мя бы́стро убега́ет,

Но в душе́ ого́нь живёт.

Э́та ночь нас окрыля́ет,

Пусть она́ не пропадёт!

Эй, подру́ги, не проща́емся,

Пусть запо́мнится моме́нт!

Мы танцу́ем, улыба́емся,

Пусть нам све́тит лу́нный свет.

Translation

Verse 1

The stars shine brightly in the sky,

The warm wind is calling us.

The streets are glowing once again,

The city lives in joy.

Pre-Chorus

We are walking, we are laughing,

This night is burning for us.

Music laughs all around,

Everything spins and shines!

Chorus

Hey, my friends, time is up,

Soon a new day will come!

But for now, we keep on dancing,

Let the moonlight shine on us.

Verse 2

The sky is full of bright lights,

The voice of the streets is a rhythm.

We will remember this evening,

Like a sweet, warm poem.

(Pre-Chorus + Chorus)

Bridge

Time is running fast,

But fire still lives in our souls.

This night lifts us up,

Let it never fade away!

Hey, my friends, we won't say goodbye,

Let's remember this moment!

We are dancing, we are smiling,

Let the moonlight shine on us.

Song Title

The title **Ты – моё сéрдце** means "You are my heart."
It's a simple sentence, but a great example of how personal and possessive pronouns work in Russian.

Let's break it down:

- Ты – you (informal, singular; nominative case)
- моё – my (neuter form of мой)
- сéрдце – heart (neuter noun)

Possessive Pronouns in the Song

Why моё and not мой or моя?

Because in Russian, **possessive pronouns** must agree in **gender**, **number**, and **case** with the noun they describe.

In the title **Ты – моё сéрдце**, the noun **сéрдце** (heart) is **neuter**, so the pronoun must also be neuter: **моё**.

Here's a quick review with examples:

Gender/Number	my	your	Example
Masculine	мой	твой	мой друг (my friend)
Feminine	моя́	твоя́	твоя сестра (your sister)
Neuter	моё	твоё	моё сердце (my heart)
Plural	мои	твои	твои друзья (your friends)

Note: The forms for **твой** are exactly like **мой**, just swap out the м for **тв**.

Exercise: Choose the correct form of **мой** or **твой** to match the noun. (All nouns are in the nominative case.)

1.   ___ ма́ма (my mom)
2.   ___ окно́ (your window)
3.   ___ брат (my brother)
4.   ___ друзья́ (your friends)
5.   ___ се́рдце (my heart)
6.   ___ го́род (your city)
7.   ___ маши́на (my car)
8.   ___ де́ло (your business)

Answers: 1. моя́ 2. твоё 3. мой 4. твой 5. моё 6. твой 7. моя́ 8. твоё

Personal Pronouns in the Song

Here's a quick-reference chart showing all the **first- and second-person singular** pronouns used in the song, with **English translations**:

Case	I	you
Nominative	я (I)	ты (you)
Genitive	меня́ (of me)	тебя́ (of you)
Accusative	меня́ (me)	тебя́ (you)
Dative	мне (to me)	тебе́ (to you)
Instrumental	мной (with me)	тобо́й (with you)

You'll spot several of these in the song. For example:

- Без тебя́ – without you (genitive)
- Меня́ нет – I don't exist (genitive after нет)
- Я люблю́ тебя́ – I love you (accusative)
- С тобо́й – with you (instrumental)
- Мне бо́льно – It hurts me / I feel pain (dative)

Exercise: Choose the correct form of the first- or second-person singular pronoun based on the context.

1. Я люблю́ ___ (you)
2. Без ___ мне грустно. (you)
3. Ты зна́ешь ___? (me)
4. Мне ну́жен ___ сове́т. (your)
5. С ___ мы пое́дем на мо́ре. (you)
6. Покажи́ ___ фотогра́фии. (me)
7. Где ___? Я тебя́ не ви́жу! (you)
8. Ты скуча́ешь по ___? (me)

Answers: 1. Я люблю́ тебя́ – love takes the accusative 2. Без тебя́ мне грустно – без requires the genitive 3. Ты зна́ешь меня́? – know takes the accusative 4. Мне ну́жен твой сове́т – your advice → possessive твой, совет is masculine 5. С тобо́й мы пое́дем на мо́ре – с (with) takes the instrumental 6. Покажи́ мне фотогра́фии – show (to) me → dative 7. Где ты? Я тебя́ не ви́жу! – see takes the accusative 8. Ты скуча́ешь по мне? – the preposition по takes the dative

Understanding how these forms work is essential, not just for grammar, but for expressing emotion clearly in Russian. And as this song shows, you'll use them a lot.

Listen to the song once all the way through. Just relax and absorb it. As you listen, try to notice when the speaker says **"I"** and **"you"**, and see if you can hear how the pronouns change depending on the line.

Key_Words_

This song uses **simple words** to express deep emotion: words like сердце, свет, больно, and любовь. You may already know many of them, but can you **catch them when you hear them**?

Listen with the Word Cloud

To help you train your ear, we've created a **word cloud** (on the next page) using **all the words from the song lyrics**. The words are randomly placed, but the ones used most frequently appear largest.

1. **Take a moment to review the word cloud.**
   Look for words you recognize. Take note of larger words. They appear more often in the lyrics.
2. **Now listen to the song.**
   As you listen, **circle any words you hear** in real time. Listen carefully. Some words may go by quickly or be pronounced differently in the melody.
3. **Repeat if you want!**
   Listening more than once is a great idea. You'll likely hear more words each time. This activity helps you tune your ear to **recognize even the words you thought you knew.**

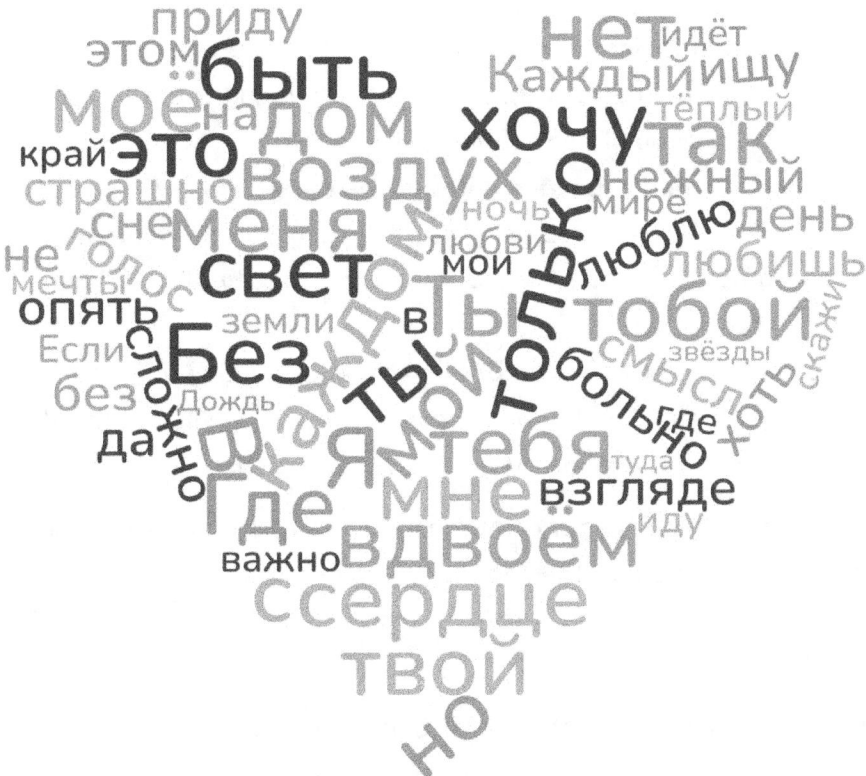

This is a great warm-up before reading the lyrics. You'll be surprised how much you recognize once you've given your ears a chance to adjust!

Next up, we'll take a closer look at the lyrics themselves.

First Look at the Lyrics

Well! You've already seen all the lyrics... just in a very different format, **scattered in a word cloud**.

Now it's time to see them in order, in their full emotional context.

Here's your step-by-step:

1. **Listen to the song again while reading along with the lyrics** (on page 100). You'll probably recognize many words you already circled. Nice work!
2. **Now read the lyrics without the music.** Take your time. Focus on the meaning of each line. Try to figure out as much as you can **without** looking at the English translation.
3. **After that, read the English translation.** See how close you were! Don't worry if some parts still feel unclear. We'll explore them line by line in the **Breakdown** section next.

This process builds your comprehension skills step by step, and you'll get more out of the song each time you revisit it.

Breakdown

Let's take a close look at how the song works, line by line. This section explains vocabulary, verb forms, cases, and phrasing to help you better understand and appreciate both the language and the emotion.

Verse 1

Ка́ждый день без тебя́ – э́то ночь

- **Ка́ждый день** – every day (каждый = every; день = day, masculine nominative)
- **без тебя́** – without you (без requires the genitive case of ты → тебя)
- **э́то ночь** – this is night; simple noun–noun structure

Без любви́ в э́том ми́ре мне бо́льно

- **без любви** – without love (любовь → любви, genitive)

- **в этом мире** – in this world (в + мир in prepositional: мире)
- **мне больно** – it hurts me (impersonal: мне = dative; больно = painful)

Где ты? Где твой тёплый го́лос?

- **где ты?** – where are you?
- **твой тёплый голос** – your warm voice (твой = your; тёплый = warm; голос = voice, masculine)

Я ищу́, но опя́ть мне так сло́жно

- **я ищу** – I search / I'm searching (1st person singular, present of искать)
- **но опять** – but again
- **мне так сложно** – it's so difficult for me (impersonal; мне = dative; так сложно = so hard)

Chorus

Ты – моё се́рдце, ты – мой свет

- **моё сердце** – my heart (сердце is neuter → моё)
- **мой свет** – my light (свет is masculine → мой)

Без тебя́ меня́ нет

- **без тебя** – without you (genitive)
- **меня́ нет** – literally "there is no me" (impersonal structure)

Ты – мой во́здух, ты – мой дом

- **воздух, дом** – masculine nouns; мой is used both times
  - **воздух** – air
  - **дом** – home

Я хочу́ быть с тобо́й вдвоём

- **я хочу** – I want (1st person singular, present of хотеть)
- **быть с тобой** – to be with you (с + тобой = instrumental)
- **вдвоём** – together, just the two of us (adverb used only for two people)

Verse 2

В ка́ждом взгля́де – твой не́жный свет

- **в каждом взгляде** – in every glance (взгляд = glance; в + prepositional = взгляде)
- **твой нежный свет** – your gentle light

В ка́ждом сне – то́лько ты, то́лько ты

- **в каждом сне** – in every dream (сон → сне, prepositional)
- **только ты** – only you

Éсли лю́бишь, скажи́ мне «да»

- **если любишь** – if (you) love (2nd person singular of любить)
- **скажи мне** – tell me (imperative of сказать)

Я приду́, хоть на край земли́

- **приду** – I will come (future tense of прийти)
- **хоть** – even (used for emphasis)
- **на край земли** – to the edge of the earth (край = edge, земли = genitive of земля)

Bridge

Дождь идёт, но мне не стра́шно

- **дождь идёт** – it's raining (идти used for weather)
- **мне не страшно** – I'm not afraid (impersonal construction)

Я иду́ туда́, где ты

- **иду** – I go, I'm going (1st person singular, present of идти)
- **туда, где ты** – there, where you are (туда = to there)

Я люблю́ тебя́ – э́то так ва́жно

- **люблю тебя** – I love you (тебя = accusative)
- **это так важно** – this is so important (impersonal: важно = important)

Ты – мой смысл, мои́ звёзды, мечты́

- **мой смысл** – my meaning (**смысл** = meaning, masculine)
- **мои звёзды, мечты** – my stars, my dreams (plural nouns; **мои** = plural "my")
- You are my meaning, my stars, my dreams – A poetic line using concrete imagery for abstract emotion

Lyrics_

Куплёт 1

Ка́ждый день без тебя́ – э́то ночь,

Без любви́ в э́том ми́ре мне бо́льно.

Где ты? Где твой тёплый го́лос?

Я ищу́, но опя́ть мне так сло́жно.

Припёв

Ты – моё се́рдце, ты – мой свет,

Без тебя́ меня́ нет.

Ты – мой во́здух, ты – мой дом,

Я хочу́ быть с тобо́й вдвоём.

Куплёт 2

В ка́ждом взгля́де – твой не́жный свет,

В ка́ждом сне – то́лько ты, то́лько ты.

Е́сли лю́бишь, скажи́ мне «да»,

Я приду́, хоть на край земли́.

(Припе́в)

Бридж

Дождь идёт, но мне не стра́шно,

Я иду́ туда́, где ты.

Я лю́блю тебя́ – э́то так ва́жно,

Ты́ – мой смысл, мой звёзды, мечты́.

(Припе́в)

Translation

Verse 1

Every day without you is like night,

Without love, this world just feels painful.

Where are you? Where's your warm voice?

I keep searching, but it's so hard again.

Chorus

You are my heart, you are my light,

Without you, I don't exist.

You are my air, you are my home,

I want to be with you alone.

Verse 2

In every glance, your gentle light,

In every dream, only you, only you.

If you love me, say "yes,"

I will come, even to the world's end.

(Chorus)

Bridge

The rain falls, but I'm not afraid,

I go to where you are.

I love you; it means so much,

You're my meaning, my dreams, my stars.

(Chorus)

TRACK 10

Это мой день

Song Title
Copulas in Russian

The title of the song is simple, but it gives us a great opportunity to look at a unique feature of Russian grammar: **Russian doesn't use a verb for "to be" in the present tense.**

In English, we'd say **"This is my day."**

That little word **"is"** is called a **copula.** It links the subject and the description.

In Russian, though, **no verb is needed in the present tense.** You simply put the two parts of the sentence together:

- **Это мой день** = "This – my day" → This is my day.

There's no word for "is" here because Russian doesn't use it in the present tense.

Compare:

- **Это мой друг.** → This is my friend.
- **Москва́ — столи́ца Росси́и.** → Moscow is the capital of Russia.
- **Он учи́тель.** → He is a teacher.

Notice: no **есть**, no verb at all!

In the past or future tense, Russian does use forms of "to be" (like был, будет, etc.). But in the present tense, there's no word for "am, is, are" because they simply don't exist in Russian.

So... when do we see the dash (—)?

In Russian, a **dash (—)** is often used to show the connection between two nouns (or a noun and a pronoun) when there's no verb in the present tense.

- **Э́то — мой день.** (This is my day.)
- **Она́ — учи́тель.** (She is a teacher.)
- **Москва́ — столи́ца Росси́и.** (Moscow is the capital of Russia.)

The dash is **optional** in many simple sentences, especially in casual writing or speech, but it's commonly used when:

- Both sides of the sentence are **nouns** or **pronouns**
- You want to **emphasize** the connection or structure
- You're writing more formally... or in song lyrics, for rhythm

So in this song, **"Э́то мой день"** skips the dash, but it could just as easily be written "Э́то — мой день" with the same meaning.

First Listening

Before you start focusing on individual words or grammar, just **listen to the song all the way through** once.

As you listen, ask yourself:

- What kind of day is she describing?
- What mood or feeling does the song give you?
- Do you recognize any familiar words or phrases?

Don't worry about understanding everything. This first listen is just about **getting a feel** for the rhythm, tone, and everyday life described in the lyrics.

Ready? Hit play and enjoy!

Key_Words_

Imperfective and Perfective Verbs

This song follows a typical day, from morning routine to evening relaxation, and it gives us a great chance to observe **how Russian uses verb aspects** to describe different kinds of actions.

Imperfective Verbs = Ongoing or Repeated Actions

Most of the verbs in the song are **imperfective**. That's because they describe **routine** or **habitual** actions, things the speaker does regularly, or activities that are in progress when we "see" them in the song.

For example:

- я проыпа́юсь (I wake up)
- я чи́щу зу́бы (I brush my teeth)
- я слу́шаю му́зыку (I listen to music)

These aren't dramatic, one-time events. They're just part of everyday life.

Perfective Verbs = One-Time, Completed Actions

But not everything in the song is repetitive! The speaker also mentions a few **specific, completed actions**, things that will happen once and be done.

Here are three key perfective verbs in the song:

- **я закажу́** (I will order) – ordering soup and salad (a single, future action)
- **мы обсу́дим** (we'll discuss) – having one specific conversation
- **я куплю́** (I'll buy) – buying something tasty later

These **perfective verbs** are used in the **future tense** to express **intentions or plans**: actions the speaker expects to complete once.

Compare: Imperfective vs. Perfective

Imperfective Verbs – describe regular, repeated, or ongoing actions:

- **просыпа́юсь** (I wake up) → from просыпа́ться – used for the speaker's daily routine
- **чи́щу** (I brush) → from чи́стить – brushing teeth, a repeated morning habit
- **слу́шаю** (I listen) → from слу́шать – ongoing action (listening to music on the metro)

Perfective Verbs – describe single, completed actions (often in the future):

- **закажу́** (I will order) → from заказа́ть – ordering one specific meal at the café
- **обсу́дим** (we'll discuss) → from обсуди́ть – one planned conversation during lunch
- **куплю́** (I'll buy) → from купи́ть – one-time action: picking up something tasty for dinner

Listen again and try to catch these verbs. Pay attention to how **imperfective verbs** create a sense of **routine and flow**, while the **perfective verbs** highlight **moments of change, choice, or intention**.

This is one of the most powerful tools in Russian grammar, and songs like this one show how naturally it works in context.

First Look at the Lyrics

You've come a long way! This final song is a chance to put your skills into action, but also to try out new ways of working with Russian lyrics that you can use on your own in the future.

Here's how to get the most out of the lyrics (on page 112) this time:

Listen while reading along in Russian.
Focus on the connection between sound and spelling. Do you recognize where the stress falls? Which endings are easy to catch? Or tricky?

Read the lyrics slowly, without the music.
Try to say them out loud. Practicing pronunciation without the singer's rhythm can help you internalize natural stress and phrasing.

Use your grammar brain.
Pick out verbs, cases, or pronouns you recognize, especially ones we've reviewed throughout this book. Don't worry about full sentences; find the patterns.

Guess the meaning from context.

What's happening in each verse? Can you identify the tone: relaxed, rushed, joyful?

Now check the English translation.

Compare your guesses. Where were you close? Where did Russian surprise you?

Then listen again, eyes closed.

You've seen the text. Now focus purely on the sound. How much can you catch this time?

Breakdown

Verse 1

Ýтро тёплое, буди́льник звени́т

- **утро** – morning (neuter, nominative)
- **тёплое** – warm (adjective, neuter, agreeing with утро)
- **будильник** – alarm clock (masculine, nominative)
- **звенит** – (it) rings (3rd person singular, present tense, imperfective)

Я просыпа́юсь, но хочу́ ещё спать

- **просыпаюсь** – I wake up (1st person singular, reflexive, imperfective)
- **хочу** – I want (1st person singular, present tense)
- **ещё спать** – to sleep more (infinitive спать = to sleep; ещё = still/more)

Тяну́сь к телефо́ну – пять но́вых сообще́ний

- **тянусь** – I reach (1st person singular, reflexive, imperfective)

- **к телефону** – toward the phone (preposition к + dative case)
- **пять** – five (numeral)
- **сообщений** – messages (plural, genitive; required after numbers above four)

Но вре́мени нет, мне пора́ встава́ть

- **времени нет** – there's no time (genitive времени used for absence)
- **мне пора** – it's time for me (мне = dative, impersonal phrase)
- **вставать** – to get up (imperfective infinitive)

Чи́щу зу́бы, принима́ю душ

- **чищу** – I brush (1st person singular, present tense, imperfective)
- **зубы** – teeth (plural, accusative)
- **принимаю душ** – I take a shower (literally "receive a shower")

На ку́хне варю́ кре́пкий чёрный ко́фе

- **на кухне** – in the kitchen (prepositional case)
- **варю** – I brew (1st person singular, imperfective; literally "boil/cook")
- **крепкий чёрный кофе** – strong black coffee (all masculine, accusative)

Где моя́ блу́зка? Ах, вот же она́!

- **моя блузка** – my blouse (feminine, nominative)
- **вот же она** – oh, here it is! (used for sudden realization)

Быстро одéться – и в óфис

- **быстро одеться** – to get dressed quickly (одеться = perfective infinitive, reflexive)
- **и в офис** – and [off] to the office (accusative case after в used for destination)

Chorus

Э́то мой день, всё идёт, как всегдá

- **это мой день** – this is my day (present tense copula omitted, as explained earlier)
- **всё идёт** – everything is going (идти, imperfective)
- **как всегда** – as always

Не скýчно, не я́рко, но мне хорошó

- **не скучно / не ярко** – not boring / not bright (short-form neuter adjectives, impersonal)
- **мне хорошо** – I feel good (impersonal expression)

Э́то мой день – он простóй, но роднóй

- **он простой** – it is simple (простой = masculine adjective)
- **но родной** – but familiar/dear (родной = native, emotionally close)

И в нём есть теплó и немнóго мечты́

- **в нём** – in it (prepositional, masculine/neuter)
- **есть** – there is (used when something exists or is present)
- **тепло** – warmth (neuter noun)
- **немного мечты** – a little bit of dream (мечта in genitive singular after немного)

Метро́ перепо́лнено, лю́ди молча́т

- **метро переполнено** – the metro is crowded (short-form passive adjective)
- **люди молчат** – people are silent (молчат = 3rd person plural, imperfective)

Я слу́шаю му́зыку в ста́рых нау́шниках

- **слушаю музыку** – I listen to music (accusative case)
- **в старых наушниках** – in old headphones (prepositional plural)

На рабо́те табли́цы, звонки́ и отчёты

- **на рабо́те** – at work (prepositional)
- **таблицы, звонки и отчёты** – spreadsheets, calls, and reports (nominative plural list)

Обе́денный переры́в – мой час свобо́ды

- **обеденный перерыв** – lunch break
- **мой час свободы** – my hour of freedom

В кафе́ закажу́ себе́ суп и сала́т

- **в кафе** – at a café
- **закажу** – I will order (заказать, perfective)
- **себе** – for myself (dative reflexive)
- **суп и салат** – soup and salad (accusative)

С подру́гой обсу́дим после́дние но́вости

- **с подругой** – with a (female) friend (instrumental case)
- **обсудим** – we'll discuss (обсудить, perfective)
- **последние новости** – the latest news

Час пролета́ет – обра́тно к дела́м

- **час пролетает** – an hour flies by (пролетает = imperfective, present)
- **обратно к делам** – back to work (literally "back to tasks")

Но ве́чер уже́ бли́зко

- **вечер близко** – evening is near
- **уже** – already

Verse 3

Ве́чером йо́га, пото́м магази́н

- **вечером** – in the evening (instrumental case for time expression)
- **йога, потом магазин** – yoga, then the store

Куплю́ что́-то вку́сное, сде́лаю у́жин

- **куплю** – I will buy (купить, perfective)
- **что-то вкусное** – something tasty
- **сделаю ужин** – I will make dinner (сделать, perfective)

Фильм, кни́га, немно́го вина́

- **немного вина** – a little wine (genitive after немного)

А за́втра всё бу́дет так же

- **а завтра** – and tomorrow
- **всё будет** – everything will be (future tense)
- **так же** – the same

Lyrics

Утро тёплое, будильник звенит,

Я просыпаюсь, но хочу ещё спать.

Тянусь к телефону – пять новых сообщений,

Но времени нет, мне пора вставать.

Чищу зубы, принимаю душ,

На кухне варю крепкий чёрный кофе.

Где моя блузка? Ах, вот же она!

Быстро одеться – и в офис.

Припев

Это мой день, всё идёт, как всегда,

Не скучно, не ярко, но мне хорошо.

Это мой день – он простой, но родной,

И в нём есть тепло и немного мечты.

Куплет 2

Метро переполнено, люди молчат,

Я слушаю музыку в старых наушниках.

На работе таблицы, звонки и отчёты,

Обеденный перерыв – мой час свободы.

В кафе закажу себе суп и салат,

С подругой обсудим последние новости.

Час пролетает – обратно к делам,

Но вечер уже близко.

(Припев)

Ве́чером йо́га, пото́м магази́н,

Куплю́ что́-то вку́сное, сде́лаю у́жин.

Фильм, кни́га, немно́го вина́,

А за́втра всё бу́дет так же.

(Припе́в)

Translation

Verse 1

A warm morning, the alarm clock rings,

I wake up, but I want to sleep more.

I reach for my phone – five new messages,

But no time, I have to get up.

Brush my teeth, take a shower,

Brew strong black coffee in the kitchen.

Where's my blouse? Oh, here it is!

Get dressed quickly – and off to the office.

Chorus

This is my day, everything goes as usual,

Not boring, not bright, but I feel good.

This is my day – it's simple, but mine,

And there's warmth in it and a little bit of dreams.

Verse 2

The metro is crowded, people are silent,

I listen to music in my old headphones.

At work, spreadsheets, calls, and reports,

Lunch break – my hour of freedom.

At a café, I'll order soup and a salad,

Chat with my friend about the latest news.

An hour flies by – back to work,

But evening is getting closer.

(Chorus)

Yoga in the evening, then the store,

I'll buy something tasty, make dinner.

A movie, a book, a little wine,

And tomorrow will be the same.

(Chorus)

lingualism

Visit our website for information on current and upcoming titles and free language learning resources.

www.lingualism.com